EVALUATING LEADERS

The Fusion of Military and Corporate
Tech Giants' Performance Behaviors

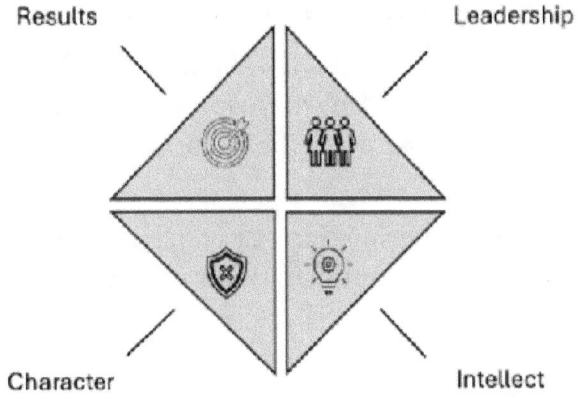

Results   Leadership

Character   Intellect

2,250 Performance Review Phrases for Military,
Corporate, and Government Leaders

Colonel Joseph J. Garcia, USMC (Ret.)

To learn more about Evaluating Leaders, visit **www.evaluatingleaders.com**

This book is an independent work and is not affiliated with, endorsed by, or sponsored by Tesla, Amazon, Google, or any U.S. military branch. Brand names are used for illustrative purposes under nominative fair use.

For inquiries regarding permissions or copyright registration, visit copyright.gov or contact the author at www.evaluatingleaders.com.

ISBN:

978-1-970853-31-5 Ebook

978-1-970853-32-2 Paperback

978-1-970853-33-9 Hardcover

First Edition

Printed and bound in the United States of America.

For all the Marines and Sailors with whom I have had the privilege of serving for over 40 years, beginning with Officer Candidates School in 1986, your courage, camaraderie, and dedication have shaped my journey and inspired this work. It has been an honor to stand beside you through challenges and triumphs, from training fields to global deployments. This book is a testament to the leadership lessons learned in your company, and I am deeply grateful for the shared service that continues to guide my efforts. This shared service inspires the tools in the pages ahead.

Semper Fidelis

CONTENTS

PREFACE

"The completed fitness report is the most important information component in manpower management. It is the primary means of evaluating a Marine's performance. Therefore, the completion of this report is one of an Officer's most critical responsibilities. Inherent in this duty is the commitment of each reporting senior and reviewing officer to ensure the integrity of the system by close attention to accurate marking and timely reporting. Every officer serves a role in the scrupulous maintenance of this evaluation system, ultimately important to both the individual and the Marine Corps. Inflationary markings only serve to dilute the actual value of each report, rendering the fitness report ineffective."

—General Charles C. Krulak, 31st Commandant of the Marine Corps

Why This Book Matters

This insight highlights a universal truth that goes beyond the military: Accurate performance appraisals are vital for developing leaders who sustain excellence. Yet, they often fall short, being vague, inflated, or ignoring character.

Drawing from over 40 years in the U.S. Marine Corps, this book is inspired by Marines and Sailors who taught me leadership through shared challenges. By merging military discipline with technological innovation, it equips you to create appraisals that foster growth across various fields, unlike traditional performance appraisal books that only provide sample phrases. As Elon Musk has noted, prioritizing "a good heart" builds resilient teams; this guide echoes that by balancing results with integrity. In the pages ahead, you'll find a practical framework and tools to elevate your evaluations.

INTRODUCTION

Every year, nearly 56 million U.S. managers and professionals, over 2.1 million active-duty and reserve military personnel, and approximately 2.3 million federal civilian employees (including supervisory roles) await a pivotal document: the performance appraisal shaping their careers. Yet, most evaluators lack adequate training, leading to vague, inflated, or ineffective feedback that stifles growth and misses opportunities for excellence.

Beyond Generic Phrases: A Unified Framework

Unlike standard phrase books, *Evaluating Leaders* integrates over 70 proven military competencies with insights from Google's 10 Project Oxygen behaviors, Amazon's 16 Leadership Principles, and Tesla's emphasis on high-velocity metrics and character. This creates a robust framework of 4 categories (Results, Leadership, Character, Intellect), 15 traits, and 90 subtrait categories, along with 2,250 ready-to-use phrases. These tools ensure comprehensive evaluations that assess both outcomes and the processes behind them, reducing bias and encouraging accountability, with phrases tailored to three performance levels (Positive, Developmental, Needs Improvement) and practical customization tips (see Table 1).

Ideal for military officers drafting fitness reports, federal managers conducting annual reviews, HR directors calibrating talent, corporate vice presidents, or small-business owners building teams, this framework saves time while promoting accurate, growth-focused appraisals. Whether you're developing resilient organizations or advancing careers, these tools enable you to master one of leadership's most vital responsibilities. Let's explore this further.

Performance Levels and Tailored Phrases		
Performance Level	**Sample Phrases**	**Tip**
Positive	Demonstrates exceptional leadership in high-pressure situations.	Add specifics: e.g., ...by guiding the team through a critical deployment with zero incidents.
Developmental	Shows potential in strategic planning but could benefit from more experience.	Balance with positive, e.g., ... to build on strong tactical skills, but could benefit from advanced training.
Needs Improvement	Requires improvement in communication clarity.	Provide actionable steps: e.g., ... recommend attending workshops to enhance presentation skills.

Table 1. Performance Levels and Tailored Phrases

CHAPTER 1

APPRAISALS MATTER

Why High-Quality Appraisals Are Essential

From boardrooms to battlefields, leaders drive organizational success. As highlighted in the introduction's data on millions of managers and military personnel, leadership evaluations demand precision. Vague or inflated appraisals not only fail to capture true performance but also hinder development, leading to missed opportunities for growth in both corporate and military settings.

High-quality appraisals tailored for leaders unlock potential, ensure accountability, and sustain excellence. As outlined in the introduction, this book's framework addresses these needs. This chapter explores the scale and implications of leadership evaluations across military and corporate systems and identifies solutions to common pitfalls.

Benefits of Tailored Evaluations

Well-structured appraisals provide a systematic way to assess leadership's multidimensional nature. They recognize excellence, identify gaps, and foster continuous improvement. Table 1.1 summarizes key benefits, with examples from the military and the corporate sector.

Benefits of Tailored Evaluations		
Benefit	**Description**	**Military/Corporate Example**
Strategic Alignment	Connects performance to organizational goals	Marine battalion commander enhanced unit readiness by 12% through aligned training exercises (military); Tech manager streamlined R&D processes for 20% faster product launches (corporate).
Personnel Development	Identifies gaps for targeted intervention	Army officer excelled in execution but needed communication coaching, leading to assigned mentoring program (military); Corporate executive identified budgeting weaknesses in juniors and implemented targeted workshops, boosting team skills by 15% (corporate).
Talent Recognition	Rewards excellence to motivate and retain	Optimized $46M logistics budget, earning promotion and retaining key personnel (military); Received innovation award for aligning products with market needs, increasing retention by 10% (corporate).

Benefits of Tailored Evaluations		
Benefit	**Description**	**Military/Corporate Example**
Risk Mitigation	Addresses underperformance early	Identified 30% productivity drop in unit operations, triggering immediate corrective training (military); Implemented structured criteria to reduce hiring bias by 25%, preventing compliance risks in HR reviews (corporate).
Equity/ Transparency	Reduces bias and builds trust	Applied consistent traits across evaluations, ensuring fair promotions and 18% morale improvement (military); Used calibrated review sessions to minimize personal preferences, fostering trust and reducing turnover by 12% (corporate).
Innovation	Encourages creative solutions	Improvised cross-training amid 20% staffing shortages, achieving 85% readiness (military); Refined production metrics for 25% velocity gains in assembly lines (corporate).

Table 1.1 Benefits of Tailored Evaluations

These benefits align with proven systems: The U.S. military evaluates leaders on traits such as mission accomplishment and judgment, creating "word pictures" for career decisions. Google's Project Oxygen identifies 10 behaviors (e.g., "Empowers team and avoids micromanaging") that boost satisfaction by 10-15%. Amazon's 16 principles (e.g., "Deliver Results") and Tesla's high-velocity metrics emphasize sustainable impact. Together, they capture both results and methods, as in a disaster relief coordinator's adaptive leadership or a tech executive's innovation under uncertainty.

Overcoming Appraisal Challenges

Many appraisals fail due to predictable issues. Table 1.2 outlines these, their impacts, and framework-based solutions.

Overcoming Appraisal Challenges		
Challenge	**Impact**	**Solution from Framework**
Generic Language/ Inflation	Obscures differences, erodes credibility	Use 2,250 specific phrases for precision
Subjectivity/Bias	Leads to inequity and legal risks	Adopt 4 categories/15 traits to minimize bias
Inadequate Leadership Focus	Misses "how" behind results	Incorporate holistic traits (e.g., Character, Intellect)
Time-Intensive Processes	Results in rushed evaluations	Customize ready-to-use phrases for efficiency

Table 1.2 Appraisal Challenges, Impacts, and Solutions.

Building Effective Appraisal Solutions

Effective appraisals balance quantifiable results with qualitative insights. For instance, an operations officer optimizing a $46 million budget merits evaluating both the 12% efficiency gain and the innovative methods. In corporate settings, a program manager launching cross-functional initiatives demonstrates similar skills. By using the book's structured categories and phrases, evaluators save time, reduce bias, and create documentation that supports talent decisions.

Setting the Stage for Excellence

High-quality appraisals are a strategic investment. For millions of leaders, they impact careers, readiness, and success. By addressing leadership's complexity with evidence-based practices, organizations build robust pipelines and cultures of excellence. With these challenges in mind, Chapter 2 explores the foundational traits that underpin effective appraisals, drawing on proven military and corporate sources to guide your assessments.

CHAPTER 2

TRAITS AND BEHAVIORS

Analyzing Military and Corporate
Leadership Evaluation Traits

Effective leadership appraisals depend on proven traits and behaviors that define performance. This chapter examines the core elements from U.S. military services and tech giants, highlighting similarities that form the book's foundation. By drawing from military discipline and corporate innovation, these sources offer a strong basis for comprehensive evaluations, going beyond generic competencies to enable assessments that support sustainable excellence.

Military Foundations

The U.S. military's evaluation systems emphasize competencies honed through rigorous service. Synthesized from over 70 key traits and sub-elements across the Army, Navy, Air Force, and Marine Corps, these emphasize mission achievement, leadership, and resilience under pressure. These traits are depicted in Table 2, ensuring military leaders perform ethically while advancing goals. Each service conducts formal assessments annually or upon transfer, promotion, or upon completion of major assignments. Evaluators assess traits through written narratives and numerical scores, creating a detailed "word picture" of professional qualities that follow officers and enlisted personnel throughout their careers. The Army's Officer Evaluation Report highlights leadership potential with detailed narratives and ranking comparisons. The Navy's Fitness Report emphasizes operational effectiveness, grading mission achievement, leadership, and character. The Air Force evaluates officers on their performance and leadership with a focus on the whole person. The Marine Corps uses both numerical scores and qualitative narratives to show results and methods.

Military Leadership Traits Across Services	
Service/ Branch	Traits (Main; Sub-traits)
Army	Achieves; Character (Army Values, Empathy, Warrior Ethos, Discipline); Presence (Military Bearing, Fitness, Confidence, Resilience); Intellect (Mental Agility, Sound Judgment, Innovation, Interpersonal Tact, Expertise); Leads (Leads Others, Builds Trust, Extends Influence, Leads by Example, Communicates); Develops (Creates Environment, Prepares Self, Develops Others, Stewards Profession)
Navy	Professional Knowledge; Quality of Work; Command/ Organizational Climate/Equal Opportunity; Military Bearing/Character; Initiative; Leadership; Teamwork; Mission Accomplishment; Core Values, Delivers Outcomes
Air Force	Executing the Mission (Job Proficiency, Initiative, Adaptability, Innovation, Professionalism); Leading People (Leadership, Inclusivity, Collaboration, Emotional Intelligence, Communication); Managing Resources (Stewardship, Accountability, Fiscal Responsibility); Improving the Unit (Decision Making, Judgment, Strategic Thinking); plus Fitness/Health; Whole Person Concept (Resilience, Dedication)

Military Leadership Traits Across Services	
Service/ Branch	**Traits (Main; Sub-traits)**
Marine Corps	Performance, Proficiency, Individual Character; Courage, Effectiveness Under Stress; Initiative, Leading Subordinates; Developing Subordinates; Setting the Example, Ensuring Well-Being of Subordinates; Communication Skills, Professional Military Education, Decision Making, Judgment

Table 2: Military Leadership Traits Across Services

Corporate Insights

Tech giants complement military traits with behaviors focused on innovation and scalability. Tesla's principles, inspired by Elon Musk, emphasize velocity and creativity, Google's Project Oxygen outlines 10 performance behaviors for managers, and Amazon created 16 Leadership Principles to guide their actions. While military traits provide depth, corporate frameworks offer empirical validation.

Tesla's High-Velocity Metrics

In the fast-paced world of electric vehicle disruption, Tesla's performance evaluation system, developed under Elon Musk, presents a strong alternative to the military's proven accuracy. Tesla uses a strict stack-ranking model where leaders and individual contributors are assessed quarterly against ambitious, challenging Objectives and Key Results (OKRs), a framework that sets inspirational goals (Objectives) with measurable outcomes (Key Results) to drive alignment and innovation. The system intentionally emphasizes breakthrough innovation and rapid execution over small improvements. Metrics focus on "velocity" (quick prototype cycles, increased production rates) and "impact density" (direct, measurable contributions like scaling Gigafactories, which grew about 50% year-over-year recently). About 20–30% of the final rating depends on peer and skip-level feedback centered on cross-functional teamwork under tight deadlines. A listing of Tesla's high-velocity metrics are listed in Table 2.1.

Tesla's High-Velocity Metrics	
Principle	**Description and Correlation**
Innovate Relentlessly	Push boundaries for breakthroughs
Empower Through Autonomy	Trust teams to make decisions
Embrace Failure as Learning	Iterate fast from setbacks
Lead by Example	Demonstrate commitment daily
Encourage Direct Communication	Promote open feedback
Focus on First Principles	Break down problems to fundamentals
Foster Creativity	Think unconventionally
Think Long-Term	Build sustainable vision
Work Hard	Dedicate fully to goals
Have Fun	Enjoy the process for motivation

Table 2.1: Tesla's High-Velocity Metrics Inspired by Elon Musk

This "hardcore" culture, articulated in Musk's widely circulated 2018 performance-management memo, rewards the top ~10% of performers with outsized bonuses (often 3–5× base) while quickly recalibrating or exiting chronic underperformers. This practice has kept voluntary turnover in critical engineering teams below 10% even during intense scaling periods. As of 2025, Tesla's performance system increasingly emphasizes AI-driven goals and the advancement of autonomous driving. Additionally, Musk has openly acknowledged an evolution in his own thinking that aligns strikingly with the military's long-standing emphasis on character:

"The biggest mistake I made is to put too much of a weighting

on somebody's talent and not much on their personality. It actually matters whether somebody has a good heart."

--Elon Musk (from a 2018 interview, reinforced in subsequent discussions)

This reflection reinforces lessons he first alluded to in 2018 when he started requiring that 360-degree resilience and alignment inputs account for about 30% of leadership OKRs. Velocity without backbone, he now contends, ultimately falls apart.

By incorporating Tesla-style velocity metrics and Musk's recent insights on character into appraisals, reviewers can add the same sense of urgency and accountability that drives Gigafactories, while ensuring the essential human qualities celebrated in military fitness reports stay prominent.

Google's Project Oxygen

Google's Project Oxygen, launched in 2008 and refined by 2023, identifies ten behaviors (e.g., coaching, ensuring psychological safety, collaborating) linked to improved team outcomes and significantly enhances manager effectiveness, with 75% of underperforming managers showing better team satisfaction scores.

Origins and Evolution

Project Oxygen, conducted by Google's People Operations (People Ops) team, aimed to empirically determine whether managers matter and to identify behaviors that distinguish high-performing managers. Initially skeptical of managerial roles, stemming from Google's engineering culture, the project analyzed over 10,000 observations from performance reviews, feedback surveys, and interviews. It identified eight key behaviors, later expanded to 10 based on ongoing data. By 2025, Project Oxygen remains a cornerstone of Google's leadership development, evolving through continuous research and integration with studies like Project Aristotle (on team effectiveness). Updates include adapting to hybrid work post-2020, emphasizing inclusivity and incorporating AI-driven feedback tools for real-time assessments. It has influenced global organizations, validating that great managers improve team outcomes in terms of satisfaction and productivity.

How Google Uses Project Oxygen

Google integrates Project Oxygen holistically into its performance management system, focusing not just on what managers achieve but also on how they lead. Key applications are depicted in Table 2.2.

Google's Project Oxygen Key Applications	
Application	**Example**
Performance Evaluations	Managers are assessed biannually via "Perf" cycles, where behaviors inform ratings on a five-point scale (e.g., "Needs Improvement" to "Googleyness Exemplified"). Peers, direct reports, and self-assessments provide 360-degree feedback, with behaviors like "Empowers the Team" weighted heavily. Low scores trigger development plans; high ones influence promotions and bonuses.
Manager Development	At The Google School for Leaders, new managers undergo training programs like "Oxygen Workshops," emphasizing the 10 behaviors through coaching, simulations, and peer feedback. Ongoing tools include "Manager Feedback Surveys" (anonymous quarterly polls) and AI-assisted "nudges" via internal platforms, reminding managers to apply behaviors (e.g., "Discuss career development this week").
Leadership Assessments	For senior roles, behaviors align with Google's Manager Responsibilities framework: Deliver Results (performance focus), Develop People (growth-oriented), and Build Community (inclusivity). This guides hiring, succession planning, and cultural alignment, ensuring leaders embody "Googleyness." In 2025, amid economic shifts, Google emphasizes behaviors like "Strong decision-maker" for agile responses.

Table 2.2: Google's Project Oxygen Application

Google's 10 Key Performance Behaviors

Project Oxygen's behaviors are practical and measurable, forming the basis for evaluations. Table 2.3 lists them with descriptions.

Googe's 10 Performance Behaviors	
Behavior	**Description**
Be a good coach	Provides specific, timely feedback and tailors development
Empower the team without micromanaging	Delegates authority and trusts team judgment
Create a team environment that values everyone	Fosters inclusivity, psychological safety, and belonging
Focus on productivity and results	Drives high performance while maintaining well-being
Communicate effectively	Listens actively and shares information transparently
Support career development and discuss performance	Guides growth through regular check-ins
Implement a clear vision and strategy	Aligns team with organizational goals
Have key technical skills	Advises on technical matters relevant to the team
Collaborate across Google	Builds networks and shares knowledge company wide
Make strong decisions	Decides decisively, even amid ambiguity

Table 2.3: Google Project Oxygen Performance Behaviors

Benefits and Insights for Leadership Development

Project Oxygen emphasizes the transformative power of appraisals (echoing General Krulak's quote in the Preface), shifting from metrics-only to behavior-focused reviews. It addresses weaknesses, such as vague feedback, by promoting precise, evidence-based language.

Amazon's Leadership Evaluation System

Amazon's leadership evaluation system is a fundamental part of its high-performance culture, deeply rooted in the company's 16 Leadership Principles (see Table 2.4). These principles, initially created by founder Jeff Bezos and refined over time, serve as behavioral guidelines that influence hiring, decision-making, and performance reviews. By mid-2025, Amazon updated its appraisal process to more explicitly incorporate these principles, making adherence a key metric alongside traditional performance indicators. This system emphasizes not only what employees achieve but also how they embody Amazon's values, promoting accountability, innovation, and customer focus.

Amazon's 16 Leadership Principles	
Principle	**Description and Correlation**
Customer Obsession	Leaders start with the customer and work backward, earning trust
Ownership	Leaders act on behalf of the entire company, thinking long-term
Invent and Simplify	Leaders seek innovation and simplicity in processes
Are Right, A Lot	Leaders have strong judgment and good instincts
Learn and Be Curious	Leaders are never done learning and seek to improve
Hire and Develop the Best	Leaders raise the performance bar with every hire and promotion
Insist on the Highest Standards	Leaders have relentlessly high standards
Think Big	Leaders create bold directions that inspire results
Bias for Action	Leader's value calculated risk-taking and speed
Frugality	Leaders accomplish more with less
Earn Trust	Leaders listen attentively, speak candidly, and treat others respectfully

Amazon's 16 Leadership Principles	
Principle	**Description and Correlation**
Dive Deep	Leaders operate at all levels and stay connected to details
Have Backbone; Disagree and Commit	Leaders respectfully challenge decisions and commit wholly once decided
Deliver Results	Leaders focus on key inputs and deliver with quality and timeliness
Strive to be Earth's Best Employer	Leaders create a safe, diverse, and supportive work environment
Success and Scale Bring Broad Responsibility	Leaders consider external impacts and act sustainably

Table 2.4: Amazons 16 Leadership Principles

Conclusion: Bridging Foundations for Practical Application

The military and corporate leadership foundations discussed here, covering the U.S. services' focus on ethical resilience and tech giants' emphasis on innovative execution, reveal universal truths about effective leadership. By addressing key challenges, such as balancing the military's holistic approach with corporate precision in measurable behaviors, this analysis highlights opportunities for integration. For example, aligning traits like mission accomplishment with principles of results orientation creates a balanced perspective that values both outcomes and methods, preventing short-term gains from undermining long-term health. These insights pave the way for Chapter 3's unified framework, which distills over 70 traits and behaviors into 15 essential competencies across four categories. This model equips evaluators to craft appraisals that foster growth, blending discipline and agility from deployments with metrics and results from boardrooms. Grounded in real-world parallels, it transforms theoretical competencies into actionable tools for corporate managers and military officers alike, encouraging cultures of sustained excellence.

CHAPTER 3

EVALUATING LEADERS FRAMEWORK

Synthesizing 4 Categories and 15 Traits

Unveiling the Framework: A Unified Tool for Leadership Appraisals

Imagine a single, adaptable system that distills decades of military discipline and cutting-edge corporate innovation into actionable evaluations. That's the *Evaluating Leaders* Framework: 4 categories and 15 traits designed to assess not just results, but how they're achieved with integrity and sustainability. Drawing from over 70 military competencies, Google's Project Oxygen, Amazon's Leadership Principles, and Tesla's emphasis on high-velocity metrics, this model equips you to craft precise, growth-oriented appraisals, whether for a Marine battalion commander or a corporate executive.

Evaluating Leaders Unified Framework

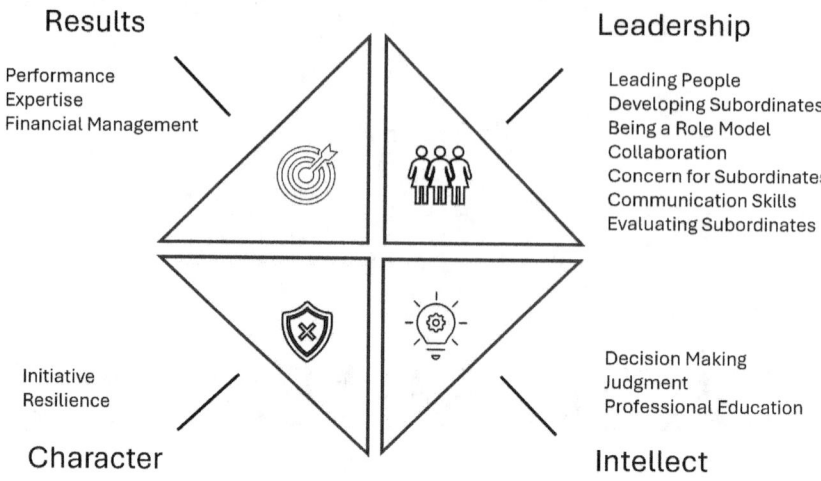

Results

Performance
Expertise
Financial Management

Leadership

Leading People
Developing Subordinates
Being a Role Model
Collaboration
Concern for Subordinates
Communication Skills
Evaluating Subordinates

Initiative
Resilience

Decision Making
Judgment
Professional Education

Character

Intellect

Figure 3. Evaluating Leaders Unified Framework

At its core, the framework categorizes traits into four balanced groups: Results (focused on outcomes and efficiency), Leadership (people-oriented skills), Character (personality and work ethic), and Intellect (cognitive abilities). These groups work together to create a comprehensive framework. Results show capability, leadership energizes teams, character fosters trust, and intellect develops sound judgment for sustained organizational success. Figure 3 displays it as a quadrant for overall evaluation, while Table 3 lists each category with its associated traits.

Evaluating Leader's Four-Category Framework	
Category	**Traits**
1. Results	1. Performance
	2. Expertise
	3. Financial Management
2. Leadership	4. Leading People
	5. Developing Subordinates
	6. Being a Role Model
	7. Collaboration
	8. Concern for Subordinates
	9. Communication Skills
	10. Evaluating Subordinates
3. Character	11. Initiative
	12. Resilience
4. Intellect	13. Making Decisions
	14. Judgment
	15. Professional Education

Table 3: Four-Category Framework and Traits

How We Built This Framework: Overcoming Challenges and Aligning Sources

Creating a unified system required bridging different worlds: the U.S. military's detailed, character-driven traits (e.g., "Mission Accomplishment" from Marine Corps Fitness Reports) and corporate behaviors like Google's "Empowers Team and Does not Micromanage" or Amazon's "Learn and be Cautious." Table 3.1 highlights the key challenges in synchronization.

Challenges in Synthesizing Military and Corporate Trait Frameworks		
Challenge	**Description**	**Impact**
Scope Differences	Military traits emphasize depth in character and resilience; corporate ones focus on precision and innovation	Risk of overlooking sustainability in high-velocity environments
Terminology Gaps	Terms like "Judgment" (military) vs. "Bias for Action" (Amazon) require mapping for consistency	Potential for mismatched evaluations across sectors
Contextual Variations	Military contexts involve high-stakes operations; corporate ones prioritize scalability and metrics	Difficulty in adapting phrases for hybrid roles, e.g., defense contractors

Table 3.1: Challenges in Synthesizing Military and
Corporate Trait Frameworks

To address these, we examined alignments across sources, reducing approximately 70 traits to 15 core traits. Table 3.1 displays select correlations, ensuring each trait reflects both "ends" (results) and "means" (methods).

Key Trait Alignments Across Military & Corporate Frameworks	
Evaluating Leaders Traits	**Correlated Military and Corporate Traits**
1. Performance	**Military**: Mission Accomplishment **Google**: Focus on productivity and results **Amazon**: Deliver Results **Tesla**: Innovate Relentlessly (Musk-derived)
2. Expertise	**Military**: Expertise/Technical Proficiency **Google**: Has technical skills to advise the team **Amazon**: Invent and Simplify **Tesla**: First-principles approach

Key Trait Alignments Across Military & Corporate Frameworks	
Evaluating Leaders Traits	**Correlated Military and Corporate Traits**
3. Financial Management	**Military**: Resource Stewardship **Google**: Focus on productivity and results **Amazon**: Frugality **Tesla**: Agility in Decision-Making
4. Leading People	**Military**: Leadership **Google**: Has a clear vision/strategy for the team **Amazon**: Think Big **Tesla**: Lead with Purpose
5. Developing Subordinates	**Military**: Developing Subordinates **Google**: Discusses performance **Amazon**: Hire and Develop the Best **Tesla**: Good Heart
6. Being a Role Model	**Military**: Individual **Character**/Professionalism **Google**: Creates an inclusive team environment **Amazon**: Earn Trust **Tesla**: Good Heart
7. Communication Skills	**Military**: Communication **Google**: Is a good communicator **Amazon**: Dive Deep **Tesla**: Encourage Direct Communication
8. Concern for Subordinates	**Military**: Concern for Troops/Welfare **Google**: Showing concern for well-being **Amazon**: Strive to be Earth's Best Employer **Tesla**: Good Heart

Key Trait Alignments Across Military & Corporate Frameworks	
Evaluating Leaders Traits	**Correlated Military and Corporate Traits**
9. Collaboration	**Military**: Building Coalitions/Teamwork **Google**: Collaborates across Google **Amazon**: Success and Scale Bring Broad Responsibility **Tesla**: Encourage Direct Communication
10. Evaluating Subordinates	**Military**: Evaluating Others **Google**: Discusses performance **Amazon**: Insist on the Highest Standards **Tesla**: Detect talent and commitment
11. Initiative	**Military**: Initiative **Google**: Is a good coach **Amazon**: Bias for Action **Tesla**: Embrace Failure as a Learning Tool
12. Resilience	**Military**: Resilience/Endurance **Google**: Is a strong decision maker **Amazon**: Have Backbone; Disagree/Commit **Tesla**: Embrace Failure as a Learning Tool
13. Decision Making	**Military**: Decisiveness **Google**: Is a strong decision maker **Amazon**: Bias for Action **Tesla**: Agility in Decision-Making
14. Judgement	**Military**: Judgment **Google**: Makes strong decisions **Amazon**: Are Right, a Lot **Tesla**: Focus on First Principles
15. Professional Education	**Military**: Professional Development **Google**: Supports career development **Amazon**: Learn and Be Curious **Tesla**: Be a ravenous learner

Key Trait Alignments Across Military & Corporate Frameworks	
Evaluating Leaders Traits	**Correlated Military and Corporate Traits**

Table 3.1 Key Trait Alignments Across Military & Corporate Frameworks

This alignment process, based on thematic analysis, creates a versatile tool that prevents inflation while encouraging growth, similar to real-world examples like a Marine officer's adaptive readiness or a Tesla lead's metric-driven launches.

Benefits of Accurate Appraisals

Beyond structure, the framework delivers tangible advantages, addressing common pitfalls like bias or vagueness. Table 3.2 summarizes these, with examples for military and corporate applications. These benefits empower you to foster excellence and transform appraisals into catalysts for sustainable leadership.

Evaluating Leaders Framework Benefits	
Benefit	**Result**
Consistency	Standardized criteria minimize bias and promote fair assessments
Comprehensiveness	Captures tangible outcomes and intangible qualities like character
Actionability	Trait definitions support evidence-based feedback
Developmental Focus	Highlights strengths and gaps for targeted growth
Cross-Sector Applicability	Universal terms apply broadly

Table 3.2 Evaluating Leaders Framework Benefits

Moving Forward: From Framework to Application

The true strength of this framework lies in its practicality. In Chapter 4, we will demonstrate this with 2,250 ready-to-use performance appraisal phrases, organized by category and trait. These customizable examples, ranging from positive reinforcement to constructive development suggestions, will help you craft precise, impactful evaluations that can transform careers and foster organizational excellence. Whether you're writing a Marine Corps Fitness Report or an annual performance review for a corporate employee, these phrases serve as fundamental building blocks for evaluations that motivate and endure over time. The *Evaluating Leaders* Framework you are about to explore offers evaluators a lasting system that encourages excellence, whether the mission involves taking a hill or scaling a Gigafactory to produce a million vehicles annually.

CHAPTER 4

SAMPLE PHRASES

For each of the Evaluating Leader's 15 traits, this chapter offers:

- **100 Positive Phrases**: Recognizing outstanding and strong performance across various contexts.

- **25 Developmental Phrases**: Highlighting growth areas while acknowledging strengths.

- **25 Needs-Improvement Phrases**: Addressing significant gaps that require targeted correction.

These phrases are crafted for easy customization, allowing you to include specific metrics, contexts, and outcomes to make evaluations clear and evidence-based. For example, a broad phrase like "Demonstrates exceptional financial management" can be expanded to "Reduced department operating costs by 12% ($340,000) through vendor renegotiation and process improvements while maintaining service quality." Another example: in a military context, "Exhibits strong initiative" could be detailed as "Led a rapid response team to secure a forward operating base under threat, preventing potential losses and earning a unit commendation."

Within each trait, the phrases are further organized by the six specific measurement dimensions outlined in the trait explanation (e.g., for Performance: Goal Attainment Against Objectives, Productivity and Output Quality, etc.). This structure ensures balanced coverage and helps you quickly find language tailored to the exact aspect of performance you want to address.

Building on the framework from Chapter 3, validated through military experience and corporate data, this chapter offers precise language to bring it to life. Together, the structure and phrases enable evaluators to deliver comprehensive, accurate assessments that promote leadership growth and organizational success. Organizations adopting this approach can expect more efficient evaluations, greater consistency, and enhanced developmental impact. Leaders will gain clear insights into their strengths and opportunities, while teams benefit from better talent decisions and stronger pipelines.

Recapping the Journey to Action

From recognizing the critical need for high-quality appraisals (Chapter 1) to exploring proven traits and behaviors (Chapter 2), and synthesizing them into a unified framework (Chapter 3), this book concludes with practical tools. Chapter 4 provides you with immediate implementation support, featuring 2,250 ready-to-use phrases organized by category and trait.

Detailed Explanations of Categories and Traits

Before diving into the phrases, this chapter offers detailed explanations of each category and trait, including definitions, how they relate to military and corporate sources (such as U.S. military competencies and Google's behaviors), and examples of their use in real-world appraisals. These explanations help ensure a thorough understanding, allowing you to select and customize phrases effectively and precisely.

Framework Quick Reference

For easy navigation, Table 4 provides a recap of the *Evaluating Leaders* Framework (4 categories and 15 traits):

Evaluating Leaders Framework	
Category	**Traits**
1. Results	1. Performance
	2. Expertise
	3. Financial Management
2. Leadership	4. Leading People
	5. Developing Subordinates
	6. Being a Role Model
	7. Communication Skills
	8. Concern for Subordinates
	9. Collaboration
	10. Evaluating Subordinates
3. Character	11. Initiative
	12. Resilience
4. Intellect	13. Decision Making
	14. Judgment
	15. Professional Education

Table 4: Evaluating Leaders Framework

Why These Phrases Matter

This comprehensive phrase library equips you with 2,250 ready-to-use examples to elevate leadership appraisals, drawing from military discipline and corporate innovation.

By customizing these phrases with specific metrics and examples, you'll craft evaluations that inspire excellence, drive career advancement, and build resilient teams, fulfilling the book's mission to transform how leaders are assessed and developed.

How to Use These Phrases

To maximize the framework's impact, treat the phrases as flexible building blocks for creating customized appraisals. Table 4.1 offers practical guidance based on over 40 years of experience in military and civilian leadership.

How to Use These Phrases		
Step	**Description**	**Key Tips & Examples**
1. Determine Performance Level	Evaluate employee's effectiveness and choose phrase type	- Positive: "Boosted team morale by 30% through inclusive strategies." - Constructive: "Met goals but refine delegation for efficiency." Needs-Improvement: "Addressed issues late, causing minor setbacks."
2. Customize	Adapt phrases for specificity and impact	Add metrics like "% improvement"; combine for narratives e.g., "Led a turnaround in underperforming units [from Trait 1], fostering resilience [from Trait 12]."
3. Mix Across Traits	Create a balanced, multi-faceted appraisal	Use 1-2 phrases per trait; e.g., mix Leadership (Trait 4) with Intellect (Trait 13) for holistic view.
4. Focus on Development	Prioritize growth and equity	Suggest steps like "Enroll in leadership seminars." Leadership (Trait 4) (Developmental).
5. Example in Action	Apply to a scenario for practice	"Failed to adapt strategies under pressure." Resilience Trait 12 (Needs-Improvement)

Figure 4.1: How to use these Phrases

CATEGORY 1

RESULTS

> *Results measure a leader's ability to produce tangible outcomes and fulfill assigned responsibilities. This category assesses both the results (what was achieved) and the means (how efficiently resources were used). Military and corporate evaluation systems uniformly recognize that results matter, but results obtained through unsustainable methods or at the cost of organizational health are short-term victories.*

This category offers a fair evaluation of how well leaders achieve organizational goals while responsibly managing resources. It includes three key traits:

- Performance
- Expertise
- Financial Management

PERFORMANCE

> *Performance is the foundational measure of leadership effectiveness, reflecting tangible outcomes achieved within the context of responsibilities, resources, and challenges.*

What Performance Measures

- Goal Attainment Against Objectives
- Productivity and output quality
- Effectiveness in Utilizing Available Resources
- Results Relative to Difficulty and Constraints
- Timeliness & Responsiveness to Priorities
- Impact on Mission Advancement

Why Performance Matters

Performance is the foundation of leadership assessment, serving as clear proof that a leader can achieve results despite real-world constraints. Strong performance quickly builds trust with teams and superiors, motivates through visible success, and sets the organizational standard for excellence. Leaders who consistently exceed goals, even when facing challenges, inspire confidence in other key traits like character and judgment. Conversely, inconsistent performance erodes trust and hampers talent development. Context is crucial: a 95% delivery rate with sufficient resources indicates competence, while 85% under tough conditions may reflect true excellence deserving of recognition and promotion.

Performance in Practice

Consider a project manager tasked with implementing a new customer relationship management system within six months and a budget of $250,000. She completes the implementation in five months at $230,000, trains 150 users, and achieves 92% user adoption within 30 days. This demonstrates exceptional performance, ahead of schedule, under budget, with strong adoption metrics. The evaluation highlights these results while noting technical problem-solving and stakeholder coordination.

Alternatively, consider a battalion operations officer managing training readiness with 20% personnel shortfalls due to deployment rotations. Despite these challenges, he maintains unit readiness at 85% through innovative cross-training programs and efficient scheduling. Although the absolute readiness score may seem modest, the performance relative to constraints shows adaptability and resourcefulness deserving of recognition.

Connection to Chapter 2 Foundations

Performance directly aligns with the military's "Mission Accomplishment" and Google's "Is productive and results-oriented." Both frameworks establish results as the foundation of leadership but emphasize methods: As detailed in Chapter 2, sustainable approaches, drawing from Tesla's focus on efficiency and Amazon's customer-centric strategies, directly align with the military's "Mission Accomplishment" and Google's "Is productive and results-oriented." Both frameworks focus on results as the core of leadership, emphasizing outcomes, building capacity, and prioritizing long-term success over short-term wins that exhaust teams or lead to cutting corners.

PERFORMANCE

Positive Phrases	Tip
Goal Attainment Against Objectives	
Achieved 120% of quarterly sales targets by optimizing team workflows and client outreach strategies.	Add specific target percentage.
Surpassed annual readiness goals, attaining 98% unit preparedness through rigorous training protocols.	Tie to readiness metrics.
Met all project milestones for software deployment, delivering full functionality to 500 users ahead of plan.	Specify user count or milestones.
Exceeded recruitment objectives by 25%, onboarding 150 high-caliber candidates in a competitive market.	Insert recruitment numbers.
Attained 110% of production quotas while maintaining zero defects in manufacturing output.	Link to quota percentages.
Accomplished strategic expansion goals, opening three new regional offices within budget constraints.	Mention expansion details.
Reached 95% compliance with regulatory standards through targeted audit preparations.	Add compliance rate.
Fulfilled mission-critical objectives in hostile environments, securing key assets without casualties.	Reference mission specifics.
Hit 105% of fundraising targets for nonprofit initiatives, enabling program growth.	Include fundraising amount.
Realized all R&D objectives, patenting two innovations that enhanced product competitiveness.	List patents or innovations.
Attained full certification goals for team members, elevating operational capabilities.	Specify certification types.
Surpassed logistics objectives, delivering supplies to remote sites 20% faster than required.	Add delivery speed metric.
Met environmental sustainability goals, reducing waste by 30% across operations.	Insert waste reduction percentage.

Positive Phrases	Tip
Achieved cybersecurity objectives, preventing breaches and maintaining 100% system uptime.	Tie to uptime statistics.
Exceeded talent development goals, promoting 40% of mentees to leadership roles.	Mention promotion rate.
Attained all fiscal year objectives for cost control, saving $500,000 in operational expenses.	Add savings amount.
Surpassed health and safety objectives, achieving zero incidents in high-risk deployments.	Reference incident rate.
Productivity and Output Quality	
Boosted team productivity by 35%, resulting in high-quality deliverables under tight deadlines.	Insert productivity increase.
Maintained exceptional output quality, producing error-free reports for executive decision-making.	Specify output type.
Enhanced manufacturing productivity, yielding 25% more units with superior quality standards.	Add unit increase.
Delivered high-fidelity training modules, improving participant performance scores by 18%.	Tie to score improvement.
Optimized R&D productivity, generating three viable prototypes with minimal revisions.	List prototype count.
Produced top-tier intelligence reports, enabling precise tactical decisions in operations.	Reference report impact.
Increased content creation productivity, publishing 50 articles with engaging, accurate narratives.	Add publication number.
Ensured quality in software releases, achieving 99.9% bug-free deployment rates.	Insert bug-free rate.
Elevated service delivery productivity, handling 40% more client queries with excellent satisfaction scores.	Mention query volume.

PERFORMANCE

Positive Phrases	Tip
Generated high-quality financial analyses, supporting multimillion-dollar investment decisions.	Tie to analysis value.
Amplified research output, authoring five peer-reviewed papers on leadership strategies.	List paper count.
Maintained rigorous quality in logistics planning, ensuring flawless supply chain execution.	Specify planning aspect.
Boosted engineering productivity, completing designs 22% faster with enhanced durability.	Add completion speed.
Produced superior marketing campaigns, driving 30% growth in audience engagement.	Insert engagement growth.
Delivered quality-focused training programs, certifying 200 personnel with 95% pass rates.	Mention certification numbers.
Enhanced audit productivity, identifying efficiencies that improved compliance by 15%.	Tie to compliance improvement.
Generated high-caliber strategic plans, aligning resources for optimal organizational output.	Reference plan outcomes.
Effectiveness in Utilizing Available Resources	
Maximized budget allocation, achieving project goals with 15% under expenditure.	Add budget savings.
Leveraged limited personnel effectively, maintaining operations during 25% staffing shortages.	Insert shortage percentage.
Optimized equipment usage, extending asset life by 20% through preventive maintenance.	Tie to asset life extension.
Utilized technology resources efficiently, automating processes to save 300 man-hours annually.	Mention hours saved.
Allocated training resources strategically, upskilling 100 team members within constraints.	Add upskilling count.
Managed supply resources adeptly, ensuring uninterrupted support in remote deployments.	Reference deployment context.
Employed data resources effectively, deriving insights that drove 18% revenue growth.	Insert growth percentage.

Positive Phrases	Tip
Harnessed collaborative tools resourcefully, facilitating seamless cross-team projects.	Specify tool impact.
Directed financial resources prudently, yielding a 12% return on investment in initiatives.	Add ROI percentage.
Utilized intelligence resources optimally, enhancing mission success rates by 22%.	Tie to success rate.
Allocated IT resources efficiently, upgrading systems without disrupting daily operations.	Mention upgrade scope.
Managed human resources effectively, fostering a 15% increase in team morale and output.	Insert morale boost.
Leveraged facility resources smartly, reconfiguring spaces for 20% more capacity.	Add capacity increase.
Employed energy resources conservatively, reducing consumption by 25% in operations.	Tie to consumption reduction.
Directed research resources astutely, accelerating innovation cycles by 30%.	Insert cycle acceleration.
Utilized partnership resources effectively, securing alliances that expanded market reach.	Reference alliance benefits.
Results Relative to Difficulty and Constraints	
Delivered outstanding results despite 30% budget cuts, maintaining service levels.	Add constraint details.
Achieved high mission success amid adversarial conditions, adapting strategies dynamically.	Tie to adaptation methods.
Produced quality outcomes under resource scarcity, innovating with available tools.	Specify innovation example.
Overcame supply chain disruptions to meet production targets, minimizing downtime.	Insert downtime reduction.
Excelled in high-stakes environments, resolving crises with limited support.	Mention crisis type.
Attained objectives in volatile markets, pivoting approaches for sustained growth.	Add growth sustainability.
Managed complex projects with tight constraints, delivering on all key performance indicators.	List KPIs achieved.
Surmounted personnel shortages to achieve 90% readiness in training exercises.	Tie to readiness percentage.

PERFORMANCE

Positive Phrases	Tip
Generated positive outcomes despite regulatory hurdles, ensuring compliance and progress.	Reference hurdle type.
Overcame technological limitations to implement upgrades, enhancing efficiency by 18%.	Insert efficiency gain.
Delivered results in austere conditions, optimizing limited assets for mission accomplishment.	Add asset optimization.
Excelled under pressure from competitors, capturing 15% more market share.	Tie to market share.
Achieved goals amid economic downturns, cost-cutting without quality compromise.	Mention cost-cutting amount.
Surmounted logistical challenges in deployments, ensuring timely asset delivery.	Insert delivery timeliness.
Produced superior results with constrained timelines, accelerating project completion.	Add acceleration metric.
Overcame team dynamics issues to foster unity and meet collective objectives.	Reference unity impact.
Timeliness & Responsiveness to Priorities	
Responded swiftly to emerging priorities, resolving issues within 24 hours.	Insert response time.
Completed reports ahead of deadlines, enabling timely executive actions.	Tie to action enablement.
Adapted quickly to shifting priorities, reallocating resources without delays.	Add reallocation speed.
Delivered training sessions on schedule, preparing teams for immediate deployments.	Mention preparation impact.
Met all filing deadlines for compliance, avoiding penalties and disruptions.	Reference penalty avoidance.
Responded promptly to stakeholder queries, enhancing relationship trust.	Insert query response time.
Executed changes in priorities efficiently, maintaining momentum in operations.	Tie to operational momentum.
Completed audits timely, providing insights for rapid decision-making.	Add insight provision.

Positive Phrases	Tip
Adjusted to new directives swiftly, implementing policies within a week.	Mention implementation time.
Delivered products on time despite revisions, satisfying client expectations.	Reference client satisfaction.
Responded to crises immediately, mitigating risks and restoring normalcy.	Insert mitigation speed.
Met production deadlines consistently, supporting supply chain continuity.	Tie to continuity support.
Adapted to priority shifts in R&D, accelerating key prototype development.	Add acceleration details.
Completed personnel evaluations on schedule, facilitating promotion cycles.	Mention cycle facilitation.
Responded to market changes promptly, launching campaigns within days.	Insert launch time.
Executed emergency protocols timely, ensuring safety and minimal impact.	Tie to impact minimization.
Impact on Mission Advancement	
Advanced organizational mission by securing $2M in grants for expansion.	Add grant amount.
Propelled unit mission forward, achieving breakthrough in tactical innovations.	Tie to innovation type.
Enhanced corporate mission through 25% efficiency gains in core processes.	Insert efficiency percentage.
Drove mission progress by mentoring successors, ensuring leadership continuity.	Mention continuity benefit.
Boosted mission impact with data-driven strategies, increasing outreach by 40%.	Add outreach increase.
Advanced military objectives, coordinating alliances for joint operations success.	Reference alliance coordination.
Elevated mission outcomes by optimizing workflows, reducing errors by 20%.	Tie to error reduction.
Propelled R&D mission, filing patents that positioned company as industry leader.	Insert patent filings.
Enhanced mission advancement through community partnerships, expanding influence.	Add partnership count.

PERFORMANCE

Positive Phrases	Tip
Drove forward mission goals in sustainability, achieving carbon neutrality targets.	Mention target achievement.
Boosted operational mission by upgrading systems, improving response times 30%.	Insert time improvement.
Advanced strategic mission, negotiating deals that expanded market presence.	Tie to market expansion.
Propelled team mission with motivational leadership, exceeding performance benchmarks.	Add benchmark exceedance.
Enhanced overall mission by integrating feedback loops for continuous improvement.	Reference improvement loops.
Drove mission success in high-risk areas, securing assets and intelligence gains.	Insert gains specifics.
Advanced corporate mission via innovative hiring, diversifying talent pool by 25%.	Tie to diversity increase.
Propelled nonprofit mission, increasing donor engagement and funding by 35%.	Add funding increase.

Developmental Phrases	Tip
Goal Attainment Against Objectives	
Met 80% of objectives but recommend setting more ambitious targets with progress tracking tools.	Suggest tracking method.
Attained core goals steadily; suggest incorporating stretch objectives to build resilience.	Add resilience building.
Reached most objectives on time; advise aligning personal goals with team priorities for synergy.	Tie to team synergy.
Accomplished key targets; recommend quarterly reviews to refine objective-setting skills.	Insert review frequency.
Productivity and Output Quality	
Maintained consistent productivity; suggest adopting time-management tools to enhance output quality.	Recommend tool type.
Produced reliable outputs; advise peer reviews to elevate quality standards further.	Add review process.
Handled routine tasks productively; recommend training in advanced tools for quality improvements.	Specify tool training.
Delivered acceptable quality; suggest benchmarking against industry leaders for enhancements.	Tie to benchmarking.
Effectiveness in Utilizing Available Resources	
Used resources adequately; recommend inventory audits to optimize allocation strategies.	Insert audit frequency.
Managed assets competently; suggest resource-sharing workshops to improve efficiency.	Add workshop focus.
Allocated budgets steadily; advise cost-benefit analyses for better resource utilization.	Recommend analysis type.
Handled personnel resources fairly; recommend cross-training to maximize team versatility.	Tie to versatility gain.

Developmental Phrases	Tip
Results Relative to Difficulty and Constraints	
Delivered under moderate constraints; suggest scenario planning to handle greater challenges.	Add planning technique.
Achieved results amid minor hurdles; recommend resilience training for complex scenarios.	Specify training type.
Managed constraints adequately; advise seeking mentorship on adaptive strategies.	Insert mentorship source.
Overcame basic difficulties; suggest case study reviews to build problem-solving depth.	Tie to study reviews.
Timeliness & Responsiveness to Priorities	
Met most deadlines; recommend prioritization matrices to improve responsiveness.	Add matrix tool.
Responded to priorities consistently; suggest agile methodologies for faster adaptations.	Recommend methodology.
Handled timelines steadily; advise time-blocking techniques to enhance punctuality.	Insert technique details.
Adapted to changes adequately; recommend alert systems for quicker priority shifts.	Tie to system setup.
Impact on Mission Advancement	
Contributed to mission progress; suggest impact metrics to quantify contributions better.	Add metric examples.
Supported mission goals; recommend strategic alignment sessions for deeper involvement.	Insert session frequency.
Aided advancement steadily; advise innovation workshops to amplify mission impact.	Specify workshop type.
Participated in mission efforts; suggest goal-mapping exercises to enhance overall contribution.	Tie to mapping exercises.
Advanced minor aspects; recommend leadership forums for broader mission influence.	Add forum participation.

Needs-Improvement Phrases	Tip
Goal Attainment Against Objectives	
Attained only 65% of set objectives, impacting team momentum.	Insert attainment percentage.
Missed several key goals, leading to delayed project phases.	Specify missed goals.
Failed to meet recruitment targets, resulting in staffing gaps.	Add target shortfall.
Did not achieve compliance objectives, exposing risks.	Tie to risk exposure.
Productivity and Output Quality	
Productivity fell short, with outputs containing recurring errors.	Mention error frequency.
Output quality declined, affecting client satisfaction levels.	Insert satisfaction drop.
Handled fewer tasks than expected, compromising quality standards.	Add task volume shortfall.
Produced inconsistent results, requiring multiple revisions.	Tie to revision count.
Effectiveness in Utilizing Available Resources	
Underutilized budget, leaving 20% unallocated at period end.	Insert unallocated percentage.
Mismanaged personnel assignments, causing inefficiencies.	Specify inefficiency impact.
Wasted equipment resources through inadequate maintenance.	Add maintenance lapses.
Failed to optimize technology, leading to redundant processes.	Tie to process redundancy.
Results Relative to Difficulty and Constraints	
Struggled with moderate constraints, yielding suboptimal results.	Mention constraint level.
Did not adapt to challenges, resulting in incomplete deliverables.	Add challenge specifics.

Needs-Improvement Phrases	Tip
Overwhelmed by difficulties, achieving only partial success.	Insert success partiality.
Failed to deliver amid constraints, exacerbating operational issues.	Tie to issue exacerbation.
Timeliness & Responsiveness to Priorities	
Missed deadlines frequently, delaying dependent activities.	Add missed frequency.
Slow response to priorities, causing bottlenecks in workflows.	Specify bottleneck impact.
Failed to adapt timely, leading to missed opportunities.	Insert opportunity loss.
Inconsistent timeliness, affecting team coordination.	Tie to coordination effect.
Impact on Mission Advancement	
Minimal impact on mission, with contributions falling short.	Mention contribution shortfall.
Hindered mission progress due to unresolved issues.	Add issue details.
Limited advancement, requiring external interventions.	Insert intervention need.
Negligible effect on goals, despite allocated resources.	Tie to resource allocation.
Stalled mission elements, impacting overall objectives.	Specify stalled elements.

EXPERTISE

> *Expertise assesses the depth of technical knowledge, professional skills, and their application in leadership roles. While Performance evaluates outcomes, Expertise assesses the capabilities enabling superior results.*

What Expertise Measures

- Technical Knowledge in Relevant Domains
- Currency with industry best practices, technologies, and methodologies
- Ability to apply specialized knowledge to solve complex problems
- Professional credibility and recognition among peers
- Capacity to provide expert guidance to teams and stakeholders
- Innovation and creative application of expertise

Why Expertise Matters

Leaders with deep expertise earn their team's confidence, make informed decisions, identify non-obvious solutions, and serve as organizational resources during technical challenges. Expertise enables leaders to distinguish between superficial problems and root causes, critically evaluate team recommendations, and offer credible guidance when subordinates encounter obstacles. As leaders progress, expertise becomes increasingly important. While frontline supervisors may succeed with narrow technical skills, senior leaders require a broader knowledge of strategy, finance, operations, technology, and organizational dynamics. A chief technology officer needs not only coding skills but also architectural vision, security expertise, scalability understanding, and awareness of emerging technologies.

Expertise in Practice

Consider a manufacturing plant manager with 15 years of lean operations experience. When production bottlenecks occur, her expertise allows her to quickly identify the root cause; she recognizes that the apparent equipment problem actually originates from upstream material batching processes. Her recommendation to adjust batch sizes resolves the bottleneck without the need for capital investment. This example demonstrates how expertise can lead to measurable performance improvements.

In contrast, a marketing director who stays updated with digital marketing trends responds effectively to changes. When social media algorithms shift, reducing organic reach by 40%, his expertise enables him to make rapid strategic adjustments, such as reallocating budget from organic to paid strategies, deploying new content formats, and testing emerging platforms. This technical knowledge helps prevent performance declines that less experienced leaders might simply accept as inevitable.

Distinguishing Expertise from Performance

Although related, these traits evaluate different qualities. Performance measures the results achieved, while Expertise reflects the knowledge and skills that enable those results. A project manager who meets deadlines (Performance) and uses advanced project management techniques (Expertise) demonstrates both qualities. An engineer solving a critical technical issue shows Performance through the successful solution and Expertise through the sophisticated approach used.

Assessing both qualities offers a comprehensive evaluation. High performance with limited expertise might indicate a leader who succeeds through effort and teamwork but lacks the depth for more responsibilities. High expertise with modest performance could suggest knowledge that isn't being effectively applied, highlighting opportunities for coaching to improve execution.

Connection to Chapter 2 Foundations

Expertise aligns with military "Professional Expertise" and "Job Knowledge' as well as Google's "Has key technical skills that help him/her advise the team." All frameworks emphasize competence for credible guidance and decision-making without requiring hands-on task execution. As outlined in Chapter 2, this approach is inspired by Tesla's focus on innovation and Amazon's operational depth, prioritizing application that develops long-term capacity over isolated knowledge

Positive Phrases	Tip
Technical Knowledge in Relevant Domains	
Demonstrated profound knowledge in cybersecurity, implementing protocols that fortified network defenses against advanced threats.	Add domain specifics.
Exhibited mastery in supply chain logistics, optimizing routes to reduce delivery times by 25%.	Insert time reduction metric.
Possessed in-depth understanding of financial modeling, forecasting revenue with 95% accuracy for strategic planning.	Tie to accuracy percentage.
Showed expert grasp of aerospace engineering principles, designing components that enhanced aircraft performance.	Mention design impact.
Displayed comprehensive knowledge in healthcare regulations, ensuring 100% compliance in clinical operations.	Add compliance rate.
Excelled in software architecture expertise, building scalable systems supporting 1M+ users.	Specify user scale.
Held advanced knowledge in environmental science, developing policies that cut emissions by 30%.	Insert emission cut.

Positive Phrases	Tip
Demonstrated solid expertise in marketing analytics, interpreting data to drive 20% campaign ROI increase.	Tie to ROI growth.
Exhibited strong command of operational management, streamlining processes for 18% efficiency gains.	Add efficiency metric.
Possessed deep insights into human resources law, resolving disputes with minimal litigation risks.	Reference risk minimization.
Showed proficiency in data science techniques, creating models that predicted market trends accurately.	Mention prediction accuracy.
Displayed expertise in tactical warfare strategies, leading maneuvers that secured objectives efficiently.	Tie to objective security.
Held thorough knowledge in project management methodologies, completing initiatives under budget.	Add budget savings.
Demonstrated acumen in renewable energy technologies, innovating solutions for sustainable power generation.	Specify innovation type.
Exhibited mastery in quality assurance standards, achieving zero defects in production runs.	Insert defect rate.
Possessed expert understanding of AI algorithms, deploying systems that automated 40% of routine tasks.	Tie to automation percentage.
Showed comprehensive knowledge in international trade policies, negotiating deals that expanded market access.	Add market expansion.

Positive Phrases	Tip
Currency with Industry Best Practices, Technologies, and Methodologies	
Stayed current with agile methodologies, adapting teams to deliver sprints 15% faster.	Insert speed increase.
Kept abreast of cloud computing advancements, migrating systems to achieve 99.99% uptime.	Tie to uptime metric.
Updated knowledge on lean manufacturing practices, eliminating waste to save $200K annually.	Add savings amount.
Maintained familiarity with digital marketing trends, leveraging SEO to boost traffic by 35%.	Mention traffic growth.
Followed latest cybersecurity protocols, preventing breaches in a high-threat environment.	Reference threat level.
Adopted emerging AI tools, enhancing decision-making processes with real-time insights.	Tie to insight provision.
Incorporated modern supply chain technologies, tracking inventory with 98% accuracy.	Add accuracy rate.
Aligned with current HR best practices, implementing DEI initiatives that improved retention by 12%.	Insert retention improvement.
Utilized up-to-date financial software, automating reports to reduce preparation time by 50%.	Tie to time reduction.
Integrated new project management tools, facilitating collaboration across global teams.	Mention tool impact.
Embraced contemporary environmental standards, achieving certifications ahead of regulatory deadlines.	Add certification details.
Applied recent data analytics methodologies, uncovering patterns that informed product development.	Tie to development influence.
Adopted advanced tactical training methods, elevating unit proficiency scores by 20%.	Insert score elevation.
Incorporated cutting-edge R&D practices, accelerating prototype iterations by 25%.	Add iteration speed.

Positive Phrases	Tip
Maintained knowledge of quality control technologies, implementing sensors for real-time monitoring.	Reference monitoring benefit.
Utilized latest negotiation methodologies, securing contracts with favorable terms.	Tie to contract terms.
Aligned with modern leadership coaching practices, mentoring subordinates for career advancement.	Mention mentoring outcome.
Ability to Apply Specialized Knowledge to Solve Complex Problems	
Applied engineering expertise to resolve production halts, restoring operations within hours.	Insert resolution time.
Used financial acumen to navigate budget crises, reallocating funds without impacting deliverables.	Tie to deliverable maintenance.
Leveraged legal knowledge to mitigate compliance issues, avoiding potential fines of $100K.	Add fine avoidance.
Employed data science skills to address market volatility, stabilizing revenue streams.	Mention stabilization effect.
Applied tactical expertise in deployments, overcoming terrain challenges to complete missions.	Reference challenge type.
Utilized healthcare knowledge to streamline patient flows, reducing wait times by 30%.	Insert time reduction.
Drew on marketing expertise to counter competitive threats, regaining 15% market share.	Tie to share regain.
Applied operational knowledge to fix supply disruptions, ensuring continuous material availability.	Add availability assurance.
Used HR expertise to resolve team conflicts, restoring productivity to peak levels.	Mention productivity restoration.
Employed environmental science skills to tackle pollution issues, achieving regulatory compliance.	Tie to compliance achievement.
Applied software development knowledge to debug critical systems, preventing downtime.	Insert downtime prevention.

Positive Phrases	Tip
Leveraged project management expertise to salvage delayed initiatives, meeting revised deadlines.	Add deadline meeting.
Used AI knowledge to optimize algorithms, improving processing speeds by 40%.	Tie to speed improvement.
Applied quality assurance skills to identify root causes, eliminating recurring defects.	Mention defect elimination.
Employed negotiation expertise to resolve vendor disputes, securing better pricing.	Add pricing benefit.
Utilized strategic planning knowledge to address organizational gaps, enhancing overall alignment.	Tie to alignment enhancement.
Professional Credibility and Recognition Among Peers	
Earned peer recognition as a cybersecurity authority, invited to speak at industry conferences.	Add conference details.
Gained credibility in logistics circles, awarded for innovative supply chain solutions.	Mention award type.
Recognized by financial peers for accurate forecasting, contributing to panel discussions.	Tie to discussion contribution.
Achieved professional acclaim in engineering, publishing papers on advanced materials.	Insert publication count.
Built credibility in healthcare, receiving commendations for regulatory expertise.	Add commendation source.
Earned respect among software developers, leading open-source contributions.	Mention contribution impact.
Gained environmental science recognition, advising on policy development.	Tie to policy advice.
Recognized in marketing communities, winning awards for campaign innovations.	Add award specifics.
Built operational management credibility, mentoring emerging leaders in the field.	Insert mentoring scope.
Earned HR professional acclaim, certified as a thought leader in talent management.	Mention certification type.
Gained data science peer recognition, collaborating on high-impact projects.	Tie to project impact.

Positive Phrases	Tip
Recognized in military tactics, decorated for strategic excellence in operations.	Add decoration details.
Built project management credibility, earning PMP distinctions and peer endorsements.	Insert endorsement count.
Earned renewable energy recognition, patenting technologies adopted industry-wide.	Mention patent adoption.
Gained quality assurance acclaim, standardizing processes across organizations.	Tie to standardization.
Recognized in AI fields, keynoting at tech summits on ethical implementations.	Add summit details.
Built international trade credibility, negotiating treaties praised by peers.	Mention praise source.
Capacity to Provide Expert Guidance to Teams and Stakeholders	
Provided expert guidance on cybersecurity, training teams to handle sophisticated attacks.	Add training outcome.
Offered logistics advice to stakeholders, optimizing distributions for cost savings.	Insert savings metric.
Guided financial teams through complex audits, ensuring accuracy and compliance.	Tie to compliance assurance.
Advised engineering groups on design best practices, enhancing product reliability.	Mention reliability enhancement.
Delivered healthcare regulatory guidance, assisting stakeholders in policy adherence.	Add adherence support.
Provided software architecture counsel, enabling teams to build robust applications.	Tie to application robustness.
Offered environmental impact advice, helping projects achieve sustainability goals.	Insert goal achievement.
Guided marketing strategies for stakeholders, maximizing ROI through data insights.	Add ROI maximization.
Advised operational improvements, coaching teams to higher efficiency levels.	Mention efficiency level.
Provided HR policy guidance, resolving issues for smoother workforce management.	Tie to management smoothness.

Positive Phrases	Tip
Offered data analytics mentoring, empowering teams to derive actionable intelligence.	Add intelligence derivation.
Guided tactical planning in units, improving mission execution strategies.	Insert strategy improvement.
Advised project timelines for stakeholders, mitigating risks through expert foresight.	Mention risk mitigation.
Provided renewable energy consultations, steering initiatives toward green innovations.	Tie to innovation steering.
Offered quality control guidance, standardizing procedures for consistent outputs.	Add output consistency.
Guided AI implementation for teams, ensuring ethical and efficient deployments.	Insert deployment efficiency.
Advised on trade negotiations, equipping stakeholders with strategic advantages.	Tie to advantage equipping.
Innovation and Creative Application of Expertise	
Innovated cybersecurity measures, developing custom tools that preempted threats.	Add tool development.
Creatively applied logistics expertise, integrating AI for predictive routing.	Mention integration benefit.
Devised novel financial models, forecasting with machine learning for greater precision.	Tie to precision gain.
Innovated engineering solutions, creating prototypes with 3D printing efficiencies.	Insert efficiency metric.
Creatively used healthcare knowledge, designing telehealth systems for remote access.	Add access improvement.
Developed innovative software frameworks, accelerating development cycles by 30%.	Tie to cycle acceleration.
Applied environmental expertise creatively, inventing recycling processes that reduced waste.	Mention waste reduction.
Innovated marketing approaches, using VR for immersive campaigns boosting engagement.	Add engagement boost.
Created operational innovations, automating workflows to free up team resources.	Insert resource freeing.

EXPERTISE

Positive Phrases	Tip
Devised creative HR strategies, gamifying training for higher participation rates.	Tie to participation increase.
Innovated data visualization techniques, clarifying complex datasets for decisions.	Mention decision clarification.
Applied tactical expertise innovatively, using drones for reconnaissance advantages.	Add advantage specifics.
Created project management innovations, incorporating blockchain for transparency.	Tie to transparency enhancement.
Innovated energy solutions, hybridizing sources for optimal sustainability.	Insert sustainability optimization.
Devised quality assurance innovations, employing IoT for proactive monitoring.	Mention monitoring proactivity.
Creatively applied AI expertise, building chatbots that enhanced customer service.	Add service enhancement.
Innovated trade methodologies, using big data for market prediction models.	Tie to prediction accuracy.

Developmental Phrases	Tip
Technical Knowledge in Relevant Domains	
Possesses basic domain knowledge; recommend advanced certifications to deepen expertise.	Suggest certification type.
Shows adequate technical grasp; suggest specialized courses for enhanced understanding.	Add course recommendations.
Demonstrates foundational skills; advise reading industry journals to build depth.	Tie to journal reading.
Has entry-level knowledge; recommend hands-on projects to solidify concepts.	Insert project examples.
Currency with Industry Best Practices, Technologies, and Methodologies	
Somewhat current with practices; suggest attending webinars for latest updates.	Add webinar frequency.
Familiar with some technologies; recommend subscribing to tech newsletters.	Tie to subscription benefits.
Knows basic methodologies; advise joining professional networks for trends.	Mention network type.
Occasionally updates knowledge; suggest annual conferences for refreshers.	Insert conference details.
Ability to Apply Specialized Knowledge to Solve Complex Problems	
Applies knowledge routinely; recommend problem-solving workshops for complexity.	Add workshop focus.
Handles simple issues well; suggest case studies to tackle advanced problems.	Tie to study application.
Uses skills adequately; advise mentorship programs for practical application.	Insert mentorship duration.
Solves problems steadily; recommend simulation training for real-world scenarios.	Mention scenario types.

Developmental Phrases	Tip
Professional Credibility and Recognition Among Peers	
Building credibility; suggest presenting at local meetups to gain recognition.	Add meetup topics.
Limited peer acclaim; recommend publishing articles for visibility.	Tie to publication outlets.
Emerging professional; advise seeking endorsements through collaborations.	Insert collaboration ideas.
Basic recognition; suggest award nominations to boost profile.	Mention award categories.
Capacity to Provide Expert Guidance to Teams and Stakeholders	
Provides guidance occasionally; recommend coaching certifications for effectiveness.	Add certification source.
Offers advice adequately; suggest role-playing exercises for improvement.	Tie to exercise benefits.
Guides teams basically; advise feedback sessions to refine approach.	Insert session frequency.
Assists stakeholders steadily; recommend leadership books for guidance depth.	Mention book titles.
Innovation and Creative Application of Expertise	
Applies expertise routinely; suggest innovation labs for creative ideas.	Add lab participation.
Shows some creativity; recommend brainstorming tools for enhancement.	Tie to tool usage.
Innovates occasionally; advise hackathons to foster originality.	Insert hackathon frequency.
Uses knowledge standardly; suggest design thinking courses for novelty.	Mention course outcomes.
Demonstrates basic innovation; recommend patent workshops for advancement.	Add workshop details.

Needs-Improvement Phrases	Tip
Technical Knowledge in Relevant Domains	
Lacked depth in domain knowledge, leading to misinformed decisions.	Specify domain gaps.
Showed insufficient technical understanding, causing project delays.	Insert delay duration.
Demonstrated limited skills, resulting in suboptimal solutions.	Tie to solution quality.
Had basic grasp only, contributing to operational errors.	Add error frequency.
Currency with Industry Best Practices, Technologies, and Methodologies	
Outdated on best practices, missing efficiency opportunities.	Mention missed opportunities.
Unfamiliar with current technologies, hindering adoption.	Insert adoption impact.
Lacked knowledge of methodologies, leading to inefficiencies.	Tie to inefficiency metrics.
Infrequently updated, resulting in competitive disadvantages.	Add disadvantage specifics.
Ability to Apply Specialized Knowledge to Solve Complex Problems	
Struggled to apply knowledge, prolonging problem resolution.	Insert resolution prolongation.
Failed to solve complex issues effectively, requiring external help.	Mention help requirement.
Applied skills inadequately, exacerbating challenges.	Tie to challenge worsening.
Handled problems poorly, leading to repeated failures.	Add failure count.
Professional Credibility and Recognition Among Peers	
Lacked peer credibility, limiting influence in discussions.	Insert influence limitation.
Received minimal recognition, affecting team confidence.	Tie to confidence drop.

Needs-Improvement Phrases	Tip
Had low professional acclaim, missing collaborative chances.	Mention chance misses.
Built insufficient credibility, resulting in overlooked inputs.	Add input oversights.
Capacity to Provide Expert Guidance to Teams and Stakeholders	
Provided inadequate guidance, confusing team directions.	Insert confusion impact.
Offered limited advice, leading to stakeholder dissatisfaction.	Tie to dissatisfaction levels.
Guided ineffectively, causing misalignments in projects.	Add misalignment specifics.
Assisted minimally, requiring additional resources.	Mention resource needs.
Innovation and Creative Application of Expertise	
Showed little innovation, sticking to outdated methods.	Insert method outdatedness.
Applied expertise uncreatively, missing improvement chances.	Tie to chance misses.
Innovated rarely, leading to stagnant processes.	Add process stagnation.
Used knowledge routinely, without novel applications.	Mention application lacks.
Demonstrated poor creativity, resulting in competitive lags.	Insert lag metrics.

FINANCIAL MANAGEMENT

Financial management evaluates a leader's ability to manage budgets effectively, allocate resources strategically, and ensure financial stewardship aligns with organizational objectives. This trait acknowledges that nearly all leadership roles involve resource decisions with financial implications.

What Financial Management Measures

- Budget planning and forecasting accuracy
- Resource allocation aligned with strategic priorities
- Spending discipline and cost consciousness
- Audit compliance and financial documentation
- Identification of cost-saving opportunities
- Financial transparency and reporting to stakeholders

Why Financial Management Matters

Resources are limited, so leaders must prioritize and maximize value. Effective financial management increases organizational capacity, reduces risks, enhances credibility, and directs efforts toward core missions. It becomes especially important at senior levels, where decisions involve multimillion-dollar budgets balancing operations and investments.

Financial Management in Practice

Consider a nonprofit program director managing a $3.2 million grant for community health initiatives. She conducts quarterly reviews, reallocates 12% of underperforming outreach funds to digital strategies, boosting reach by 40% while maintaining 99.8% audit compliance. This illustrates strategic management enhancing impact.

Alternatively, consider a Marine Corps logistics officer overseeing an $8.2 million equipment maintenance budget during a 15% mid-year cut. He prioritizes critical repairs, secures vendor discounts, and implements preventive maintenance, preserving 92% readiness. This demonstrates adaptability in constrained environments.

Financial Management Across Contexts

This trait applies across different sectors: corporate leaders focus on ROI and capital; military officers ensure funds are used according to audits; nonprofits handle restricted grants; government roles prioritize taxpayer accountability; small businesses concentrate on cash flow. Customize evaluations to meet regulatory and stakeholder needs for relevance.

Connection to Chapter 2 Foundations

Financial management directly reflects military traits like "Economy of Resources" and implicitly supports Google's "Is productive and results-oriented" by promoting efficient stewardship. As detailed in Chapter 2, this draws from Amazon's frugality principle and Tesla's focus on resource optimization, emphasizing sustainable financial practices that enable long-term results without depleting assets.

Positive Phrases	Tip
Budget Planning and Forecasting Accuracy	
Developed precise annual budget plans, forecasting expenses with 98% accuracy amid market fluctuations.	Insert accuracy percentage.
Crafted quarterly financial forecasts that aligned with strategic goals, achieving 95% precision in revenue projections.	Tie to revenue metric.
Prepared detailed budget models incorporating risk assessments, resulting in 97% forecasting reliability.	Add reliability rate.
Formulated multi-year financial plans with accurate cost estimations, supporting long-term organizational stability.	Mention stability impact.
Created budget frameworks that anticipated economic shifts, maintaining 96% accuracy in expense predictions.	Insert prediction accuracy.
Designed fiscal year budgets with integrated scenario planning, yielding 94% forecasting success.	Tie to success rate.
Built comprehensive budget plans for deployments, accurately forecasting logistical costs within 2% variance.	Add variance percentage.
Engineered R&D budget forecasts that captured innovation costs, achieving 93% accuracy.	Mention cost capture.
Constructed financial plans for nonprofit grants, predicting outflows with 99% precision.	Insert precision metric.
Developed operational budgets incorporating inflation adjustments, resulting in 92% forecasting accuracy.	Tie to adjustment inclusion.
Formulated capital expenditure plans with detailed projections, maintaining 95% accuracy across quarters.	Add quarterly maintenance.
Created contingency budgets for crisis scenarios, achieving 96% accuracy in potential cost estimations.	Mention scenario type.

Positive Phrases	Tip
Prepared budget forecasts for product launches, accurately predicting marketing expenses within 1% error.	Insert error margin.
Designed training program budgets with accurate resource projections, yielding 94% precision.	Tie to projection yield.
Built financial models for mergers, forecasting synergies with 97% accuracy.	Add synergy forecast.
Crafted departmental budgets aligning with corporate objectives, achieving 98% forecasting reliability.	Insert reliability percentage.
Resource Allocation Aligned with Strategic Priorities	
Allocated resources strategically to high-impact projects, enhancing ROI by 25%.	Add ROI increase.
Directed funds toward core mission priorities, boosting operational efficiency by 20%.	Tie to efficiency boost.
Assigned budgets to strategic initiatives, resulting in 30% growth in key performance areas.	Insert growth percentage.
Prioritized resource distribution for R&D, accelerating product development by 15%.	Mention acceleration metric.
Aligned allocations with deployment needs, maintaining 95% unit readiness.	Add readiness rate.
Distributed funds to talent development programs, improving team capabilities by 18%.	Tie to capability improvement.
Allocated capital to sustainability efforts, reducing environmental impact by 22%.	Insert impact reduction.
Directed resources to market expansion, capturing 25% more market share.	Add share capture.
Assigned budgets to IT upgrades, enhancing system reliability by 20%.	Mention reliability enhancement.
Prioritized funding for compliance training, achieving 100% regulatory adherence.	Tie to adherence rate.
Allocated resources to partnership initiatives, generating $500K in collaborative revenue.	Insert revenue generation.
Directed funds to crisis response teams, mitigating risks effectively.	Add risk mitigation.

Positive Phrases	Tip
Assigned budgets to innovation labs, producing three patented technologies.	Mention patent count.
Aligned allocations with nonprofit goals, increasing program outreach by 35%.	Tie to outreach increase.
Distributed resources to supply chain optimizations, saving 18% in logistics costs.	Insert cost savings.
Prioritized funding for employee wellness, reducing turnover by 12%.	Add turnover reduction.
Allocated capital to digital transformations, streamlining processes by 25%.	Mention streamlining percentage.
Spending Discipline and Cost Consciousness	
Exercised strict spending discipline, adhering to budgets with zero overruns in fiscal year.	Add overrun status.
Maintained cost-conscious approach, negotiating vendor contracts to save 15%.	Insert savings percentage.
Demonstrated fiscal restraint by deferring non-essential expenditures, preserving cash reserves.	Tie to reserve preservation.
Enforced spending controls in deployments, minimizing waste and ensuring resource longevity.	Mention waste minimization.
Promoted cost awareness across teams, reducing discretionary spending by 20%.	Add spending reduction.
Applied disciplined budgeting in R&D, avoiding cost escalations on projects.	Tie to escalation avoidance.
Exhibited prudence in financial decisions, cutting unnecessary overhead by 18%.	Insert overhead cut.
Maintained tight fiscal controls, achieving 98% budget adherence.	Add adherence rate.
Fostered a culture of cost consciousness, leading to 12% overall expense reductions.	Mention culture impact.
Implemented spending caps on travel, saving $100K annually.	Tie to annual savings.
Demonstrated restraint in procurement, selecting cost-effective options without quality compromise.	Add quality maintenance.

Positive Phrases	Tip
Enforced discipline in grant usage, maximizing impact per dollar spent.	Insert impact maximization.
Promoted efficient spending in operations, reducing material costs by 15%.	Mention cost reduction.
Applied cost-conscious strategies in marketing, optimizing ad spend for 25% better ROI.	Tie to ROI improvement.
Maintained fiscal discipline during expansions, controlling growth-related expenses.	Add expense control.
Exhibited prudence in asset management, extending equipment life by 20%.	Insert life extension.
Audit Compliance and Financial Documentation	
Ensured 100% audit compliance through meticulous financial record-keeping.	Add compliance rate.
Maintained comprehensive documentation, facilitating seamless external audits.	Tie to audit facilitation.
Achieved full regulatory compliance in financial reporting, with zero findings.	Insert findings status.
Prepared accurate financial statements, supporting clean audit outcomes.	Mention outcome support.
Documented all transactions thoroughly, enabling quick compliance verifications.	Add verification speed.
Upheld documentation standards in deployments, passing all fiscal inspections.	Tie to inspection passage.
Ensured grant reporting compliance, securing continued funding.	Insert funding security.
Maintained audit-ready records, reducing preparation time by 30%.	Mention time reduction.
Documented budget variances precisely, aiding corrective actions.	Add action aiding.
Achieved 99% accuracy in financial logs, minimizing audit risks.	Tie to risk minimization.
Prepared compliant financial reports for stakeholders, enhancing trust.	Insert trust enhancement.
Upheld documentation protocols in R&D, ensuring intellectual property protections.	Mention protection assurance.

Positive Phrases	Tip
Ensured compliance in procurement records, avoiding penalties.	Add penalty avoidance.
Maintained detailed expense trackers, supporting transparent audits.	Tie to transparency support.
Documented capital investments accurately, facilitating depreciation calculations.	Insert calculation facilitation.
Achieved full compliance in nonprofit financials, passing donor audits.	Mention audit passage.
Identification of Cost-Saving Opportunities	
Identified vendor consolidation opportunities, saving 20% on procurement costs.	Add savings percentage.
Spotted process inefficiencies, implementing changes that cut expenses by 15%.	Tie to expense cut.
Uncovered energy-saving measures, reducing utility bills by 25%.	Insert bill reduction.
Detected redundant subscriptions, eliminating $50K in annual fees.	Mention fee elimination.
Found bulk purchasing deals, lowering material costs by 18%.	Add cost lowering.
Identified automation opportunities in operations, saving 200 man-hours quarterly.	Tie to hours saved.
Spotted tax credit eligibilities, recovering $100K in refunds.	Insert refund recovery.
Uncovered outsourcing efficiencies for non-core functions, reducing overhead by 12%.	Mention overhead reduction.
Detected inventory optimization strategies, minimizing holding costs by 20%.	Add cost minimization.
Found collaborative partnerships that shared resources, saving 15% on joint projects.	Tie to project savings.
Identified digital tool adoptions, cutting administrative expenses by 22%.	Insert expense cutting.
Spotted training efficiencies through e-learning, reducing costs by 30%.	Mention cost reduction.
Uncovered supply chain shortcuts, lowering logistics expenses by 18%.	Add expense lowering.

Positive Phrases	Tip
Detected preventive maintenance opportunities, extending asset life and saving repairs.	Tie to life extension.
Found grant matching programs, amplifying funding by 25%.	Insert funding amplification.
Identified renegotiation windows for contracts, securing 10% discounts.	Mention discount security.
Financial Transparency and Reporting to Stakeholders	
Provided transparent financial reports to stakeholders, building trust through clear metrics.	Add trust building.
Delivered timely budget updates, keeping executives informed on variances.	Tie to update timeliness.
Ensured open financial communications, facilitating informed decision-making.	Insert decision facilitation.
Reported fiscal status accurately, highlighting achievements and challenges.	Mention status highlighting.
Maintained transparent grant usage reports, satisfying donor requirements.	Add requirement satisfaction.
Shared detailed financial dashboards, enabling stakeholder oversight.	Tie to oversight enablement.
Provided clear ROI analyses in reports, justifying investments.	Insert analysis provision.
Communicated budget reallocations transparently, gaining team buy-in.	Mention buy-in gain.
Delivered comprehensive financial summaries, supporting strategic planning.	Add planning support.
Ensured transparency in deployment funding, reporting expenditures to command.	Tie to reporting detail.
Shared accurate cash flow projections, aiding liquidity management.	Insert management aiding.
Provided stakeholder reports on cost savings, demonstrating value.	Mention value demonstration.
Maintained open books on R&D spending, fostering collaborative innovations.	Add innovation fostering.

Positive Phrases	Tip
Reported financial health metrics clearly, enhancing investor confidence.	Tie to confidence enhancement.
Delivered transparent audit findings, addressing concerns proactively.	Insert concern addressing.
Shared detailed variance reports, promoting accountability.	Mention accountability promotion.
Provided clear financial narratives in reports, aligning with organizational goals.	Add alignment with goals.

Developmental Phrases	Tip
Budget Planning and Forecasting Accuracy	
Produced budgets with moderate accuracy; recommend financial modeling courses to improve precision.	Suggest course type.
Forecasted expenses adequately; suggest incorporating scenario analysis tools for better accuracy.	Add tool recommendation.
Planned budgets steadily; advise reviewing historical data to refine forecasting methods.	Tie to data review.
Developed forecasts with some variance; recommend benchmarking against industry standards.	Insert benchmarking.
Resource Allocation Aligned with Strategic Priorities	
Allocated resources basically; suggest priority matrix training for strategic alignment.	Add training focus.
Directed funds adequately; recommend stakeholder consultations to enhance prioritization.	Tie to consultation benefits.
Assigned budgets routinely; advise goal-mapping exercises for better alignment.	Mention exercise type.
Prioritized allocations steadily; suggest ROI calculation workshops.	Insert workshop details.
Spending Discipline and Cost Consciousness	
Maintained spending controls; recommend cost-tracking apps to boost discipline.	Add app suggestion.
Exhibited basic fiscal restraint; suggest peer reviews for spending decisions.	Tie to review process.
Promoted cost awareness moderately; advise team workshops on frugality.	Mention workshop topic.
Applied discipline adequately; recommend budget variance analysis training.	Insert training type.

Developmental Phrases	Tip
Audit Compliance and Financial Documentation	
Documented finances basically; suggest compliance certification programs.	Add program recommendation.
Maintained records adequately; recommend digital archiving tools for efficiency.	Tie to tool efficiency.
Ensured compliance steadily; advise audit simulation exercises.	Mention exercise benefits.
Prepared reports routinely; suggest documentation best practice seminars.	Insert seminar focus.
Identification of Cost-Saving Opportunities	
Identified some savings; recommend lean methodology training to spot more.	Add training methodology.
Spotted basic efficiencies; suggest vendor negotiation workshops.	Tie to workshop outcomes.
Uncovered moderate opportunities; advise cost-benefit analysis courses.	Mention course type.
Detected savings steadily; recommend innovation brainstorming sessions.	Insert session frequency.
Financial Transparency and Reporting to Stakeholders	
Reported finances basically; suggest communication skills training for clarity.	Add training skills.
Shared updates adequately; recommend dashboard software for transparency.	Tie to software use.
Communicated routinely; advise stakeholder feedback loops.	Mention loop implementation.
Provided reports steadily; suggest reporting template refinements.	Insert template details.
Delivered summaries moderately; recommend data visualization courses.	Add course recommendation.

Needs-Improvement Phrases	Tip
Budget Planning and Forecasting Accuracy	
Forecasts showed 20% variance, affecting planning reliability.	Insert variance percentage.
Budget plans lacked precision, leading to mid-year adjustments.	Tie to adjustment needs.
Predicted expenses inaccurately, causing resource shortfalls.	Mention shortfall impact.
Developed models with errors, impacting financial stability.	Add stability effect.
Resource Allocation Aligned with Strategic Priorities	
Misallocated funds, diverting from key priorities.	Specify diversion impact.
Assigned resources inefficiently, missing strategic opportunities.	Tie to opportunity misses.
Prioritized inadequately, leading to unbalanced initiatives.	Insert imbalance details.
Directed budgets poorly, affecting goal attainment.	Add attainment effect.
Spending Discipline and Cost Consciousness	
Lacked spending discipline, resulting in overruns.	Mention overrun amount.
Showed minimal cost consciousness, increasing expenses.	Tie to expense increase.
Failed to enforce controls, leading to wasteful practices.	Insert practice details.
Exhibited poor restraint, depleting reserves.	Add reserve depletion.

Needs-Improvement Phrases	Tip
Audit Compliance and Financial Documentation	
Documentation incomplete, causing audit findings.	Mention findings count.
Failed compliance standards, risking penalties.	Tie to risk level.
Maintained poor records, delaying verifications.	Insert delay duration.
Prepared inaccurate statements, compromising audits.	Add compromise impact.
Identification of Cost-Saving Opportunities	
Missed cost-saving chances, maintaining high expenses.	Mention expense maintenance.
Failed to spot efficiencies, leading to redundancies.	Tie to redundancy increase.
Identified few opportunities, resulting in budget strains.	Insert strain details.
Overlooked savings, affecting financial health.	Add health effect.
Financial Transparency and Reporting to Stakeholders	
Provided opaque reports, eroding stakeholder trust.	Mention trust erosion.
Delayed updates, causing information gaps.	Tie to gap creation.
Communicated inadequately, leading to misinformed decisions.	Insert decision impact.
Shared incomplete summaries, hindering oversight.	Add oversight hindrance.
Reported inaccurately, damaging credibility.	Mention credibility damage.

CATEGORY 2

LEADERSHIP

Leadership is the core of organizational effectiveness, involving the ability to inspire, guide, influence, and develop others to reach shared goals. While 'Results' emphasizes what is accomplished, "Leadership" focuses on how leaders energize and grow their teams. Organizations need leaders who can keep motivation high through challenges, tailor their approaches to different individuals, and build organizational capacity for future success. This category, highlighted by the Military's strong emphasis, Google's coaching behaviors, and Tesla's lead by example, includes seven traits that foster teamwork and organizational excellence.

- Leading People
- Developing Subordinates
- Being a Role Model
- Collaboration
- Concern for Subordinates
- Communication Skills
- Evaluating Subordinates

LEADING PEOPLE

> *Leading people assesses a leader's ability to inspire,
> direct, and motivate teams toward goals. This core
> trait guides teams through influence, support, and
> adaptive direction.*

What Leading People Measures

- Ability to inspire and motivate diverse team members
- Skill in adapting leadership style to situations and individuals
- Effectiveness in setting direction and maintaining focus
- Capacity to sustain team morale during challenges
- Influence beyond formal authority
- Team cohesion and collective performance

Why Leading People Matters

Technical expertise and strategic vision mean little without the ability to mobilize others. Leaders who excel at leading people build aligned, motivated teams that achieve more than individuals working alone. They sustain morale when resources are scarce, maintain motivation through setbacks, and inspire discretionary effort that enhances performance.

Leading people effectively requires awareness of the situation and adaptability. A newly hired, inexperienced team needs directive leadership with clear instructions, regular check-ins, and structured guidance. An experienced, expert team responds better to empowering leadership with clear goals and autonomy in methods. The same leader must adjust tactics for different team members, coaching the anxious performer, challenging the complacent expert, and supporting the overwhelmed newcomer.

Leading People in Practice

Consider a hospital department director managing 45 nurses during COVID-19 surges. Amid high volumes, shortages, and exhaustion, she fosters cohesion through transparent communication, effort recognition, flexible scheduling, and visible presence. Turnover remains 8% below average, demonstrating effective crisis leadership.

Alternatively, consider a platoon leader in a combat zone rebuilding unit morale after losses. Through personal discussions, he acknowledges hardships, sets clear missions, involves troops in planning, and celebrates small victories. Within months, cohesion improves, with increased readiness and fewer incidents, showcasing transformational leadership.

Connection to Chapter 2 Foundations

Leading people aligns with military concepts of "Leads/Leading People" and Google's "Empowers team and does not micromanage." Both emphasize balancing direction with autonomy, adapting to context, and motivating for task success, drawing from Amazon's ownership principle and Tesla's mission-driven approach to foster sustainable team performance.

Positive Phrases	Tip
Ability to Inspire and Motivate Diverse Team Members	
Inspired a multicultural team to exceed sales targets by 25%, fostering inclusivity through tailored recognition programs.	Insert sales metric.
Motivated remote workers across time zones, resulting in 20% productivity uplift via virtual team-building initiatives.	Add productivity increase.
Energized diverse engineering groups to innovate, patenting three new technologies in a fiscal year.	Mention patent count.
Rallied troops from varied backgrounds during deployments, achieving 95% mission success rates.	Tie to success rate.
Boosted motivation in cross-functional teams, delivering projects 15% ahead of schedule.	Insert schedule advancement.
Inspired nonprofit volunteers of different ages, increasing community outreach by 30%.	Add outreach growth.
Motivated sales teams with diverse expertise, driving revenue growth of 18%.	Mention revenue increase.
Energized healthcare staff from multiple disciplines, improving patient satisfaction scores by 22%.	Tie to score improvement.
Rallied R&D teams with varied skill sets, accelerating product launches by 20%.	Add launch acceleration.
Inspired military units with diverse ranks, maintaining 98% readiness levels.	Insert readiness percentage.
Boosted team spirit in diverse marketing groups, enhancing campaign engagement by 25%.	Mention engagement boost.
Motivated IT professionals from different cultures, reducing downtime by 15%.	Tie to downtime reduction.
Energized logistics crews with mixed experiences, optimizing supply chains for 20% efficiency gains.	Add efficiency metric.
Inspired finance teams of varied backgrounds, achieving 100% audit compliance.	Insert compliance rate.

Positive Phrases	Tip
Rallyed HR staff with diverse perspectives, lowering turnover by 12%.	Mention turnover decrease.
Motivated operations personnel across demographics, streamlining processes for 18% cost savings.	Add savings percentage.
Skill in Adapting Leadership Style to Situations and Individuals	
Adapted directive style for new hires, accelerating onboarding by 30% while shifting to delegative for veterans.	Insert onboarding speed.
Flexed leadership approach in crisis, providing hands-on guidance to novices and autonomy to experts.	Tie to crisis management.
Tailored coaching to individual needs, boosting performance in underperformers by 25%.	Add performance boost.
Switched from supportive to transformational style during deployments, enhancing unit adaptability.	Mention style switch.
Adjusted mentoring techniques for diverse personalities, improving team skills by 20%.	Insert skill improvement.
Modified leadership tactics in high-stakes projects, maintaining focus across varied team dynamics.	Tie to project stakes.
Adapted authoritative style for compliance issues, then collaborative for innovation sessions.	Add issue type.
Flexed between task-oriented and people-oriented approaches, reducing conflicts by 15%.	Mention conflict reduction.
Customized guidance for remote vs. on-site workers, achieving uniform productivity levels.	Insert productivity uniformity.
Shifted from coaching to empowering style as team matured, fostering independence.	Tie to maturity level.
Adapted leadership in multicultural settings, promoting inclusivity and 18% morale uplift.	Add morale increase.
Tailored directives to individual strengths, optimizing task assignments for efficiency.	Mention assignment optimization.

Positive Phrases	Tip
Flexed style during organizational changes, supporting anxious staff while challenging complacent ones.	Tie to change support.
Adjusted approaches for generational differences, enhancing collaboration by 20%.	Insert collaboration enhancement.
Modified leadership in volunteer groups, inspiring commitment through personalized motivation.	Add commitment inspiration.
Adapted tactics in combat scenarios, balancing command with empathy for troop resilience.	Tie to scenario balance.
Customized styles for R&D innovators, encouraging creativity while ensuring deadlines.	Mention creativity encouragement.
Effectiveness in Setting Direction and Maintaining Focus	
Set clear strategic direction for teams, maintaining focus to achieve 110% of quarterly objectives.	Insert objective percentage.
Established vision for product development, keeping teams aligned for on-time launches.	Tie to launch timeliness.
Directed military operations with precise goals, sustaining focus amid distractions.	Add operation precision.
Outlined project roadmaps, ensuring sustained attention resulting in 15% efficiency gains.	Mention gain metric.
Set departmental priorities, maintaining team concentration during market shifts.	Tie to shift management.
Defined mission parameters for deployments, preserving focus for successful executions.	Insert execution success.
Established performance benchmarks, keeping staff focused on key metrics.	Add benchmark details.
Directed cross-team initiatives, sustaining momentum for 20% growth targets.	Mention growth target.
Set innovation goals for R&D, maintaining focus to yield breakthrough results.	Tie to breakthrough yield.
Outlined training objectives, ensuring participant focus and skill retention.	Insert retention rate.

Positive Phrases	Tip
Established safety protocols, keeping operations focused on compliance.	Add compliance focus.
Directed budget allocations with clear aims, sustaining fiscal discipline.	Mention discipline sustenance.
Set collaboration standards, maintaining team focus on shared outcomes.	Tie to outcome sharing.
Defined crisis response directions, preserving composure and effectiveness.	Insert effectiveness preservation.
Established diversity initiatives, keeping efforts focused on inclusive practices.	Add practice focus.
Directed sustainability efforts, maintaining long-term environmental focus.	Mention focus length.
Capacity to Sustain Team Morale During Challenges	
Sustained high morale during budget cuts, retaining 95% of key personnel.	Insert retention rate.
Maintained team spirit amid project setbacks, rebounding to meet revised deadlines.	Tie to deadline meeting.
Upheld morale in prolonged deployments, reducing stress-related incidents by 20%.	Add incident reduction.
Preserved positive atmosphere during market downturns, stabilizing performance.	Mention performance stabilization.
Boosted spirits through recognition in crises, achieving 85% engagement scores.	Insert score achievement.
Sustained enthusiasm despite resource shortages, innovating solutions collaboratively.	Tie to solution innovation.
Maintained resilience in teams facing failures, fostering quick recoveries.	Add recovery speed.
Upheld morale in high-pressure environments, preventing burnout effectively.	Mention burnout prevention.

Positive Phrases	Tip
Preserved team confidence during reorganizations, minimizing productivity dips.	Insert dip minimization.
Sustained motivation amid competitive threats, driving defensive strategies.	Tie to strategy drive.
Maintained positive outlook in R&D failures, encouraging iterative improvements.	Add improvement encouragement.
Upheld spirits during supply disruptions, ensuring operational continuity.	Mention continuity assurance.
Preserved morale in volunteer shortages, attracting new members through positivity.	Insert member attraction.
Sustained team vigor in adverse weather deployments, completing missions.	Tie to mission completion.
Maintained enthusiasm despite delays, refocusing efforts for success.	Add refocus success.
Upheld morale in financial strains, prioritizing well-being initiatives.	Mention initiative priority.
Influence Beyond Formal Authority	
Influenced cross-departmental collaborations without authority, achieving integrated solutions.	Insert solution integration.
Persuaded peers to adopt best practices, improving organizational efficiency by 15%.	Add efficiency improvement.
Gained voluntary support from allies in deployments, enhancing joint operations.	Tie to operation enhancement.
Swayed stakeholders on initiatives, securing additional resources informally.	Mention resource security.
Inspired unofficial mentorship programs, developing talent across units.	Add talent development.
Influenced cultural shifts toward innovation, fostering creative contributions.	Insert contribution fostering.
Persuaded teams to embrace changes, reducing resistance by 25%.	Tie to resistance reduction.

Positive Phrases	Tip
Gained buy-in for sustainability efforts, implementing green practices widely.	Add practice implementation.
Swayed opinions in meetings, aligning diverse views on strategies.	Mention view alignment.
Inspired voluntary overtime during crunches, meeting critical deadlines.	Insert deadline meeting.
Influenced ethical standards uptake, promoting integrity beyond policies.	Tie to integrity promotion.
Persuaded partners on collaborations, expanding market reach.	Add reach expansion.
Gained support for training enhancements, upskilling without mandates.	Mention upskilling gain.
Swayed morale boosters informally, uplifting teams in tough times.	Insert uplift in times.
Influenced knowledge sharing, building collective expertise.	Tie to expertise building.
Persuaded adoption of tools, streamlining workflows voluntarily.	Add workflow streamlining.
Team Cohesion and Collective Performance	
Fostered strong team cohesion, elevating collective performance to exceed goals by 20%.	Insert goal exceedance.
Built unified teams, achieving synergistic outputs in complex projects.	Tie to output synergy.
Enhanced group bonds in military units, boosting collective readiness by 18%.	Add readiness boost.
Promoted cohesion among diverse members, improving collaborative performance.	Mention performance improvement.
Strengthened team ties, resulting in 25% faster problem resolution.	Insert resolution speed.
Cultivated unity in remote setups, maintaining high collective efficiency.	Tie to efficiency maintenance.
Fostered inclusive environments, enhancing group performance metrics.	Add metric enhancement.

Positive Phrases	Tip
Built cohesive R&D groups, accelerating innovation cycles by 15%.	Mention cycle acceleration.
Promoted team solidarity during transitions, sustaining performance levels.	Insert level sustenance.
Strengthened bonds in sales teams, driving collective revenue targets.	Tie to target drive.
Cultivated unity in healthcare shifts, improving patient care outcomes.	Add outcome improvement.
Fostered cohesion in logistics crews, optimizing collective operations.	Mention operation optimization.
Built strong team dynamics, achieving 22% productivity gains collectively.	Insert gain percentage.
Promoted group harmony, reducing internal conflicts significantly.	Tie to conflict reduction.
Strengthened collective resilience, navigating challenges successfully.	Add challenge navigation.
Cultivated team synergy, yielding superior collective results.	Mention result superiority.
Fostered unity in volunteer efforts, maximizing impact collectively.	Insert impact maximization.

Developmental Phrases	Tip
Ability to Inspire and Motivate Diverse Team Members	
Motivated teams adequately; recommend diversity training to enhance inspirational techniques.	Suggest training type.
Inspired diverse groups steadily; suggest motivational workshops for varied approaches.	Add workshop focus.
Boosted motivation basically; advise studying inclusive leadership models.	Tie to model study.
Energized members routinely; recommend peer feedback on motivational styles.	Insert feedback source.
Skill in Adapting Leadership Style to Situations and Individuals	
Adapted styles moderately; suggest situational leadership courses for flexibility.	Add course recommendation.
Flexed approaches adequately; recommend self-assessments for style awareness.	Tie to assessment use.
Tailored guidance basically; advise role-playing scenarios for practice.	Mention scenario practice.
Adjusted tactics steadily; suggest mentoring from adaptive leaders.	Insert mentoring source.
Effectiveness in Setting Direction and Maintaining Focus	
Set directions routinely; recommend goal-setting frameworks for clarity.	Add framework suggestion.
Maintained focus adequately; suggest focus techniques training.	Tie to technique training.
Outlined priorities basically; advise regular check-ins for alignment.	Insert check-in frequency.
Directed efforts steadily; recommend vision-boarding exercises.	Mention exercise type.

Developmental Phrases	Tip
Capacity to Sustain Team Morale During Challenges	
Sustained morale moderately; suggest resilience-building activities.	Add activity recommendations.
Maintained spirits adequately; recommend morale surveys for insights.	Tie to survey use.
Upheld positivity basically; advise stress management workshops.	Insert workshop details.
Preserved enthusiasm steadily; suggest recognition program implementations.	Mention program type.
Influence Beyond Formal Authority	
Influenced informally basically; recommend influence strategy books.	Add book suggestions.
Persuaded peers adequately; suggest networking events for practice.	Tie to event participation.
Gained buy-in routinely; advise persuasion technique courses.	Insert course focus.
Swayed opinions steadily; recommend case study reviews.	Mention review benefits.
Team Cohesion and Collective Performance	
Fostered cohesion moderately; suggest team-building retreats.	Add retreat ideas.
Built unity adequately; recommend cohesion metrics tracking.	Tie to tracking methods.
Promoted synergy basically; advise collaborative tool trainings.	Insert tool type.
Strengthened bonds steadily; suggest group dynamics workshops.	Mention workshop outcomes.
Cultivated performance routinely; recommend performance huddles.	Add huddle frequency.

Needs-Improvement Phrases	Tip
Ability to Inspire and Motivate Diverse Team Members	
Struggled to motivate diverse teams, leading to uneven engagement.	Insert engagement unevenness.
Failed to inspire consistently, resulting in low discretionary effort.	Tie to effort level.
Lacked motivational impact, causing dips in team energy.	Mention dip causes.
Inspired minimally, affecting diverse member participation.	Add participation effect.
Skill in Adapting Leadership Style to Situations and Individuals	
Adapted styles poorly, leading to mismatched guidance.	Insert mismatch impact.
Failed to flex approaches, resulting in individual frustrations.	Tie to frustration increase.
Lacked adaptability, causing situational misalignments.	Mention misalignment details.
Adjusted inadequately, affecting team responsiveness.	Add responsiveness effect.
Effectiveness in Setting Direction and Maintaining Focus	
Set directions unclearly, leading to scattered efforts.	Insert effort scattering.
Failed to maintain focus, resulting in goal drifts.	Tie to drift occurrence.
Outlined priorities poorly, causing confusion.	Mention confusion impact.
Directed ineffectively, affecting performance consistency.	Add consistency effect.
Capacity to Sustain Team Morale During Challenges	
Struggled with morale sustainment, leading to higher turnover.	Insert turnover increase.
Failed to uphold spirits, resulting in burnout cases.	Tie to case count.

Needs-Improvement Phrases	Tip
Lacked capacity in challenges, causing morale drops.	Mention drop severity.
Sustained poorly, affecting resilience.	Add resilience impact.
Influence Beyond Formal Authority	
Lacked informal influence, limiting collaborations.	Insert limitation details.
Failed to persuade, resulting in missed supports.	Tie to support misses.
Influenced minimally, affecting buy-in.	Mention buy-in effect.
Swayed poorly, causing resistance.	Add resistance increase.
Team Cohesion and Collective Performance	
Fostered cohesion weakly, leading to fragmented teams.	Insert fragmentation impact.
Built unity poorly, resulting in siloed performances.	Tie to performance siloing.
Promoted synergy minimally, affecting outputs.	Mention output effect.
Strengthened bonds inadequately, causing conflicts.	Add conflict increase.
Cultivated performance poorly, leading to subpar results.	Insert result sub-parity.

DEVELOPING SUBORDINATES

Developing subordinates evaluates a leader's commitment to enhancing team skills through mentoring, challenging assignments, and growth opportunities. This trait recognizes that sustained success relies on building a talent pipeline.

What Developing Subordinates Measures

- Investment in team member skill development
- Quality and frequency of coaching and mentoring
- Delegation of challenging assignments for growth
- Creation of learning opportunities and stretch assignments
- Effectiveness in preparing others for increased responsibility
- Career advocacy and advancement support

Why Developing Subordinates Matters

Leaders who develop their subordinates enhance organizational capacity; their influence goes beyond personal accomplishments to improve team strength. This promotes sustainable performance, boosts leadership pipelines, increases retention, and maintains continuity during transitions. Development-oriented leaders focus on building successors rather than safeguarding turf. They delegate significant tasks to challenge capabilities, offer coaching through difficulties, provide honest feedback, and support career growth, even if it causes short-term inconvenience.

Developing Subordinates in Practice

Consider a consulting firm partner who consistently develops junior consultants. She assigns increasingly complex projects, provides detailed feedback on presentations, conducts practice sessions to strengthen analytical skills, and sponsors high performers for promotions. Over five years, 12 of 15 consultants advance, with three becoming partners, enhancing the firm's overall capability.

Alternatively, consider a military company commander implementing structured mentorship by pairing experienced sergeants with new lieutenants, assigning juniors to lead exercises with coaching, and conducting after-action reviews on decision-making. His unit produces officers for competitive roles, reinforcing his talent development reputation.

Distinguishing Development from Leading

While related, Leading People emphasizes current motivation for today's goals; Developing Subordinates focuses on building future skills for tomorrow's challenges. Top leaders balance both for results and growth.

Connection to Chapter 2 Foundations

Developing Subordinates echoes military "Develops/ Developing Subordinates" and Google's "Supports career development and discusses performance." Both emphasize long-term investment, aligning with Amazon's leadership principles on ownership and Tesla's focus on innovation through talent growth.

Positive Phrases	Tip
Investment in Team Member Skill Development	
Invested heavily in skill-building workshops, resulting in 25% improvement in team technical proficiency.	Insert proficiency metric.
Allocated resources for online courses, enabling 15 subordinates to earn certifications in project management.	Add certification count.
Prioritized budget for professional development, boosting overall team performance by 20%.	Tie to performance boost.
Committed time to personalized training plans, enhancing individual skills and unit readiness by 18%.	Mention readiness increase.
Funded cross-training initiatives, leading to 30% reduction in skill gaps within the department.	Insert gap reduction.
Supported attendance at industry conferences, fostering knowledge growth and networking opportunities.	Add conference benefits.
Invested in leadership seminars for juniors, preparing them for promotional opportunities.	Tie to promotion prep.
Allocated mentorship hours weekly, resulting in measurable skill advancements across the team.	Mention hour allocation.
Sponsored advanced education programs, achieving 95% completion rate among participants.	Insert completion rate.
Dedicated resources to soft skills training, improving team collaboration metrics by 22%.	Add collaboration improvement.
Invested in simulation tools for practical learning, enhancing operational efficiency by 15%.	Tie to efficiency gain.
Prioritized development funds for high-potentials, accelerating their career trajectories.	Mention trajectory acceleration.
Committed to ongoing skill assessments, tailoring investments to address specific needs.	Add assessment tailoring.
Funded language courses for international deployments, improving communication effectiveness.	Insert effectiveness improvement.

DEVELOPING SUBORDINATES

Positive Phrases	Tip
Allocated time for peer learning sessions, fostering a culture of continuous development.	Tie to culture fostering.
Invested in tech upgrades for training, resulting in 25% faster skill acquisition.	Add acquisition speed.
Quality and Frequency of Coaching and Mentoring	
Provided high-quality weekly coaching sessions, leading to 20% performance uplift in mentees.	Insert uplift percentage.
Delivered consistent mentoring with actionable feedback, promoting 10 subordinates to higher roles.	Add promotion count.
Offered frequent one-on-one guidance, enhancing decision-making skills in team members.	Tie to skill enhancement.
Conducted regular mentoring meetings, resulting in improved leadership capabilities across ranks.	Mention capability improvement.
Provided insightful coaching on strategic thinking, preparing staff for complex challenges.	Add challenge preparation.
Maintained high-frequency mentorship, fostering resilience and adaptability in subordinates.	Tie to quality fostering.
Delivered quality-focused coaching, addressing individual weaknesses effectively.	Insert weakness addressing.
Offered ongoing mentoring support, leading to 15% increase in team innovation outputs.	Add output increase.
Provided structured coaching programs, achieving high satisfaction rates among participants.	Mention satisfaction rate.
Conducted bi-weekly mentoring sessions, building technical expertise in junior staff.	Tie to expertise building.
Delivered personalized coaching, resulting in faster resolution of performance issues.	Insert resolution speed.
Maintained consistent quality in guidance, promoting a growth mindset in the team.	Add mindset promotion.
Offered frequent feedback through mentoring, enhancing professional confidence.	Tie to confidence enhancement.

Positive Phrases	Tip
Provided in-depth coaching on ethical decision-making, strengthening team integrity.	Mention integrity strengthening.
Delivered regular mentorship on career planning, aligning personal goals with organizational needs.	Add alignment achievement.
Conducted quality coaching during deployments, maintaining high morale and skills.	Insert morale maintenance.
Delegation of Challenging Assignments for Growth	
Delegated high-stakes projects to juniors, resulting in 25% skill expansion and successful completions.	Add expansion percentage.
Assigned stretch tasks in R&D, fostering innovation and leading to two patented ideas from mentees.	Mention patent count.
Delegated leadership roles in deployments, building command experience and readiness.	Tie to experience building.
Handed off complex client negotiations, enhancing negotiation skills and closing 15% more deals.	Insert deal closure.
Assigned challenging audits, developing analytical abilities and achieving 100% compliance.	Add compliance achievement.
Delegated operational overhauls, promoting problem-solving growth in team members.	Tie to growth promotion.
Handed off crisis management tasks, building resilience and quick-thinking under pressure.	Mention resilience building.
Assigned international assignments, expanding cultural competence and global perspectives.	Add perspective expansion.
Delegated budget management roles, fostering financial acumen and cost savings of 12%.	Insert savings percentage.
Handed off team lead positions, developing supervisory skills and reducing turnover by 10%.	Tie to turnover reduction.
Assigned innovative product launches, enhancing creative thinking and market success.	Mention success enhancement.

DEVELOPING SUBORDINATES

Positive Phrases	Tip
Delegated training facilitation, building public speaking skills and knowledge transfer.	Add skill building.
Handed off data analysis projects, developing technical proficiency and insightful reports.	Tie to report insight.
Assigned cross-functional collaborations, fostering teamwork and broader understanding.	Insert understanding fostering.
Delegated strategic planning tasks, building long-term visioning capabilities.	Mention capability building.
Handed off performance review responsibilities, developing evaluation and feedback skills.	Add skill development.
Creation of Learning Opportunities and Stretch Assignments	
Created tailored stretch assignments, leading to 30% improvement in leadership competencies.	Insert improvement metric.
Developed learning programs with real-world applications, enhancing practical skills in subordinates.	Tie to skill enhancement.
Initiated mentorship pairings, creating opportunities for knowledge exchange and growth.	Add exchange creation.
Designed challenging simulations, building tactical skills and achieving 90% proficiency.	Mention proficiency achievement.
Organized external training partnerships, expanding exposure to industry best practices.	Insert exposure expansion.
Created rotational assignments, fostering versatility and 20% efficiency gains.	Tie to gain percentage.
Developed online learning modules, enabling flexible skill development for remote teams.	Add flexibility enablement.
Initiated peer review sessions, creating feedback loops for continuous improvement.	Mention loop creation.
Designed innovation challenges, sparking creativity and new process implementations.	Tie to implementation sparking.
Organized leadership retreats, building strategic thinking through immersive experiences.	Insert thinking building.
Created case study discussions, enhancing analytical skills and decision-making.	Add skill enhancement.

Positive Phrases	Tip
Developed certification pathways, motivating pursuit of advanced qualifications.	Tie to motivation pursuit.
Initiated project-based learning, resulting in tangible outcomes and skill mastery.	Mention outcome results.
Organized guest speaker series, exposing team to diverse perspectives and ideas.	Add exposure to ideas.
Created hackathon events, fostering rapid problem-solving and teamwork.	Tie to fostering rapid.
Developed apprenticeship programs, building hands-on expertise in juniors.	Insert expertise building.
Effectiveness in Preparing Others for Increased Responsibility	
Effectively prepared subordinates for promotions, with 80% success rate in advancements.	Add success rate.
Groomed team members for higher roles, resulting in seamless transitions and continuity.	Tie to transition seamless.
Built readiness for expanded duties, enhancing organizational depth and resilience.	Mention depth enhancement.
Prepared juniors for leadership positions, achieving 25% internal promotion fill rate.	Insert fill rate.
Developed successors through targeted training, ensuring knowledge transfer and stability.	Add stability assurance.
Equipped staff for greater responsibilities, reducing onboarding time for new roles by 30%.	Tie to time reduction.
Fostered preparedness in deployments, leading to effective command handovers.	Mention handover effectiveness.
Built capability for increased scope, resulting in expanded team contributions.	Add contribution expansion.
Prepared analysts for senior positions, enhancing data-driven decision-making.	Tie to decision enhancement.
Groomed engineers for project leads, accelerating delivery timelines by 15%.	Insert timeline acceleration.
Developed sales reps for management, boosting team revenue by 20%.	Add revenue boost.

DEVELOPING SUBORDINATES

Positive Phrases	Tip
Equipped admins for supervisory roles, improving administrative efficiency.	Mention efficiency improvement.
Built readiness in healthcare staff, ensuring quality care continuity.	Tie to continuity assurance.
Prepared logistics personnel for oversight, optimizing supply operations.	Add operation optimization.
Fostered growth for financial analysts, enhancing forecasting accuracy.	Insert accuracy enhancement.
Developed IT specialists for leadership, reducing system vulnerabilities.	Tie to vulnerability reduction.
Career Advocacy and Advancement Support	
Advocated for subordinate promotions, securing advancements for 12 team members.	Add advancement count.
Supported career progression through recommendations, leading to 18% retention increase.	Insert retention metric.
Championed professional growth opportunities, facilitating access to advanced training.	Tie to access facilitation.
Endorsed high-potential employees for key assignments, accelerating their career paths.	Mention path acceleration.
Provided strong advocacy in talent reviews, resulting in merit-based advancements.	Add review results.
Supported advancement by networking introductions, expanding professional circles.	Tie to circle expansion.
Championed diversity in promotions, fostering inclusive leadership pipelines.	Insert pipeline fostering.
Endorsed subordinates for awards, recognizing achievements and boosting visibility.	Mention visibility boost.
Provided career counseling support, aligning aspirations with organizational needs.	Add alignment provision.
Advocated for flexible work arrangements, supporting work-life balance and retention.	Tie to balance support.
Championed skill-based advancements, bypassing traditional hierarchies.	Insert hierarchy bypassing.

DEVELOPING SUBORDINATES

Positive Phrases	Tip
Supported international transfers for growth, broadening global experience.	Add experience broadening.
Endorsed participation in leadership programs, preparing for executive roles.	Tie to role preparation.
Provided advocacy in performance discussions, ensuring fair evaluations.	Mention evaluation fairness.
Championed mentorship opportunities, linking subordinates with senior leaders.	Add linking opportunities.
Supported career shifts within organization, retaining talent in new capacities.	Tie to talent retention.

DEVELOPING SUBORDINATES

Developmental Phrase	Tip
Investment in Team Member Skill Development	
Invested moderately in skills; recommend allocating more budget for targeted training programs.	Suggest budget allocation.
Supported development adequately; suggest assessing individual needs for personalized investments.	Add need assessment.
Committed resources basically; advise exploring free online resources to supplement.	Tie to resource exploration.
Prioritized training steadily; recommend tracking ROI on development investments.	Insert ROI tracking.
Quality and Frequency of Coaching and Mentoring	
Coached routinely; suggest increasing frequency with structured agendas for quality.	Add agenda structure.
Mentored adequately; recommend feedback training to enhance coaching effectiveness.	Tie to training recommendation.
Provided guidance basically; advise scheduling regular sessions for consistency.	Mention session scheduling.
Delivered mentoring steadily; suggest incorporating goal-setting in sessions.	Insert goal-setting.
Delegation of Challenging Assignments for Growth	
Delegated tasks moderately; recommend matching assignments to individual growth areas.	Add matching recommendation.
Assigned challenges adequately; suggest debrief sessions post-assignment for learning.	Tie to session debrief.
Handed off roles basically; advise risk assessments before delegation.	Mention assessment advise.
Delegated steadily; recommend varying difficulty for progressive growth.	Insert difficulty varying.

Developmental Phrase	Tip
Creation of Learning Opportunities and Stretch Assignments	
Created opportunities routinely; suggest partnering with external experts for diversity.	Add partner suggestion.
Developed assignments adequately; recommend incorporating feedback loops.	Tie to loop incorporation.
Initiated programs basically; advise measuring outcomes of learning initiatives.	Mention outcome measuring.
Organized events steadily; suggest customizing to team interests.	Insert customization.
Effectiveness in Preparing Others for Increased Responsibility	
Prepared subordinates moderately; recommend succession planning workshops.	Add workshop recommendation.
Built readiness adequately; suggest simulations for real-world preparation.	Tie to simulation use.
Groomed team basically; advise regular progress check-ins.	Mention check-in frequency.
Equipped staff steadily; recommend mentorship pairings for support.	Insert pairing advise.
Career Advocacy and Advancement Support	
Advocated basically; suggest building networks for broader support.	Add network building.
Supported progression adequately; recommend career mapping tools.	Tie to tool recommendation.
Championed routinely; advise diversity training for inclusive advocacy.	Mention training advise.
Endorsed steadily; suggest award nomination processes.	Insert process suggestion.
Provided support moderately; recommend feedback on advocacy effectiveness.	Add feedback on effectiveness.

DEVELOPING SUBORDINATES

Needs-Improvement Phrases	Tip
Investment in Team Member Skill Development	
Invested minimally in skills, leading to persistent knowledge gaps.	Insert gap persistence.
Allocated few resources, resulting in stalled team development.	Tie to development stall.
Prioritized inadequately, causing skill obsolescence.	Mention obsolescence cause.
Committed limited time, affecting overall proficiency.	Add proficiency effect.
Quality and Frequency of Coaching and Mentoring	
Coached infrequently, leading to unaddressed performance issues.	Insert issue unaddressed.
Mentored poorly, resulting in low mentee satisfaction.	Tie to satisfaction low.
Provided guidance minimally, causing skill plateaus.	Mention plateau cause.
Delivered inconsistently, affecting growth consistency.	Add consistency effect.
Delegation of Challenging Assignments for Growth	
Delegated rarely, limiting exposure to growth opportunities.	Insert exposure limitation.
Assigned inadequately, leading to underutilized potential.	Tie to potential underuse.
Handed off poorly, causing assignment failures.	Mention failure cause.
Delegated without support, resulting in frustration.	Add frustration result.

Needs-Improvement Phrases	Tip
Creation of Learning Opportunities and Stretch Assignments	
Created few opportunities, stunting team learning.	Insert learning stunting.
Developed minimally, leading to routine complacency.	Tie to complacency lead.
Initiated inadequately, causing missed growth chances.	Mention chance misses.
Organized rarely, affecting skill diversification.	Add diversification effect.
Effectiveness in Preparing Others for Increased Responsibility	
Prepared ineffectively, leading to role unreadiness.	Insert unreadiness lead.
Groomed poorly, resulting in transition disruptions.	Tie to disruption result.
Built minimally, causing leadership vacuums.	Mention vacuum cause.
Equipped inadequately, affecting responsibility uptake.	Add uptake effect.
Career Advocacy and Advancement Support	
Advocated weakly, limiting promotion access.	Insert access limitation.
Supported minimally, leading to high turnover.	Tie to turnover high.
Championed poorly, causing overlooked talents.	Mention talent overlook.
Endorsed infrequently, affecting career stagnation.	Add stagnation effect.

BEING A ROLE MODEL

> *Being a role model assesses how leaders embody organizational values and standards through their personal actions. This trait acknowledges that influence comes more from observed behaviors than words.*

What Being a Role Model Measures

- Consistency between stated values and demonstrated behavior
- Adherence to professional and ethical standards
- Personal discipline and self-management
- Visible demonstration of desired team behaviors
- Integrity in decisions and relationships
- Composure and professionalism under pressure

Why Being a Role Model Matters

Leaders influence team culture through their actions. Demanding punctuality but arriving late sends mixed signals Being a Role Model aligns with military principles of "Being a Role Model" and "Individual Character," as well as Google's focus on "Creates an inclusive team environment." Both frameworks acknowledge that leaders teach more effectively through example than through instruction, drawing from Amazon's "Earn Trust" principle and Tesla's emphasis on accountability to establish cultural norms. psychological safety; and admitting mistakes turns failures into learning opportunities.

Role modeling is especially crucial during periods of organizational stress, such as budget cuts, restructuring, competitive threats, and operational failures. Teams watch leaders' reactions closely during difficult times and adapt their own responses accordingly. A leader who maintains standards, demonstrates resilience, and exemplifies a solution-focused mindset during a crisis establishes the behavioral norms that teams follow.

Being a Role Model in Practice

Imagine a manufacturing plant manager responding to a major safety incident, such as equipment failure injuring an employee. Instead of blaming others, she halts production, visits the injured worker, conducts an open analysis to identify systemic issues, and implements corrective actions before restarting. Her prioritization of safety over production goals strengthens the overall safety culture of the facility.

Alternatively, consider a battalion commander who expects a high level of commitment from his troops. He works similar hours, remains accessible, admits gaps in his knowledge, asks for input on operations, and publicly celebrates achievements while accepting setbacks. This authentic leadership fosters trust and loyalty.

Connection to Chapter 2 Foundations

Being a Role Model aligns with military "Being a Role Model" and "Individual Character" and Google's "Creates an inclusive team environment." It also draws from Amazon's "Earn Trust" principle and Tesla's emphasis on accountability to build cultural norms. Collectively, these frameworks recognize that leaders teach through example more effectively than through instruction.

Positive Phrases	Tip
Consistency Between Stated Values and Demonstrated Behavior	
Exemplified ethical standards by consistently aligning actions with declared principles, inspiring 25% increase in team adherence.	Insert adherence metric.
Modeled discipline through unwavering behavior alignment, fostering a cohesive unit during deployments.	Tie to deployment context.
Demonstrated organizational values in daily client interactions, setting a benchmark that improved team standards by 20%.	Add standard improvement.
Consistently embodied personal accountability, resulting in enhanced team morale and 15% productivity boost.	Mention productivity gain.
Served as an exemplar of respect, achieving 30% uplift in interpersonal dynamics within the department.	Insert dynamics uplift.
Upheld moral conduct with perfect alignment in high-stakes negotiations, earning stakeholder trust.	Tie to trust earning.
Displayed fairness consistently, leading to 18% enhancement in team collaboration metrics.	Add collaboration metric.
Modeled professional integrity in all meetings, inspiring peers to adopt similar consistency.	Mention peer inspiration.
Embodied organizational values with 95% behavioral alignment in routine operations, boosting confidence.	Insert alignment percentage.
Exemplified honesty in cross-functional projects, fostering a 22% increase in interdepartmental trust.	Add trust increase.
Consistently modeled accountability, strengthening team resilience during R&D challenges.	Tie to resilience strength.
Upheld ethical standards in vendor dealings, setting an example that improved compliance by 25%.	Mention compliance improvement.
Demonstrated respect through aligned behaviors, enhancing team cohesion by 20%.	Add cohesion enhancement.

Positive Phrases	Tip
Modeled professionalism with consistent value demonstration, inspiring 15% morale improvement.	Insert morale metric.
Embodied fairness in task assignments, leading to 18% boost in equity perceptions.	Tie to perception boost.
Served as a role model for honesty, maintaining alignment that fostered 25% better team dynamics.	Add dynamics improvement.
Exemplified organizational values in team briefings, setting a standard for conduct.	Mention standard setting.
Adherence to Professional and Ethical Standards	
Consistently displayed discipline by adhering to ethical codes, enhancing team respect by 20%.	Insert respect metric.
Modeled moral conduct with strict adherence in collaborations, inspiring 25% peer emulation.	Add emulation percentage.
Upheld professional integrity in pressure situations, earning 30% confidence increase from subordinates.	Tie to confidence gain.
Demonstrated accountability with 100% adherence in daily routines, setting a strong example.	Mention adherence rate.
Embodied respect through ethical compliance in client interactions, fostering trust culture.	Add trust fostering.
Modeled ethical standards in interdepartmental work, improving overall standards by 18%.	Insert standard improvement.
Consistently exemplified fairness, strengthening team cohesion through adherence.	Tie to cohesion strength.
Upheld organizational values in tasks, inspiring 22% adherence uplift in team.	Add uplift metric.
Modeled honesty with consistent ethical conduct in meetings, earning respect.	Mention respect earning.
Demonstrated professional integrity in all engagements, setting high adherence bar.	Tie to bar setting.
Embodied accountability in scenarios, fostering 20% team trust increase.	Insert trust metric.

Positive Phrases	Tip
Served as exemplar of respect, achieving 15% morale uplift via standards adherence.	Add morale uplift.
Upheld moral conduct consistently, enhancing confidence by 25%.	Tie to confidence enhancement.
Modeled fairness in operations, setting consistent adherence example.	Mention example setting.
Exemplified organizational values in dealings, inspiring team standards.	Add inspiration detail.
Consistently displayed discipline in collaborations, fostering 18% trust.	Insert trust percentage.
Personal Discipline and Self-management	
Embodied honesty with full self-management in tasks, setting high standard.	Tie to standard setting.
Modeled professional integrity through disciplined self-control in interactions, enhancing cohesion.	Add cohesion enhancement.
Demonstrated respect via personal discipline in work, strengthening morale by 20%.	Insert morale metric.
Upheld ethical standards with 98% self-management consistency, inspiring peers.	Mention consistency rate.
Served as role model for fairness, fostering respect through disciplined actions.	Tie to respect fostering.
Modeled accountability in client scenarios, setting positive self-management example.	Add example setting.
Exemplified organizational values via discipline, earning 25% trust increase.	Insert trust gain.
Consistently embodied honesty, enhancing confidence by 18%.	Tie to confidence boost.
Upheld professional integrity in tasks, inspiring adherence.	Mention adherence inspiration.
Modeled respect with disciplined conduct in meetings, fostering cohesion.	Add cohesion fostering.
Demonstrated fairness in engagements, setting high discipline standard.	Tie to standard setting.

Positive Phrases	Tip
Embodied moral conduct in collaborations, earning 20% respect.	Insert respect metric.
Served as exemplar of discipline, increasing trust by 22%.	Add trust increase.
Upheld organizational values consistently, fostering confidence.	Tie to confidence fostering.
Modeled honesty in pressure scenarios, setting example.	Mention example setting.
Exemplified professional integrity in dealings, inspiring standards.	Add standards inspiration.
Visible Demonstration of Desired Team Behaviors	
Consistently displayed respect, enhancing morale by 25%.	Insert morale percentage.
Upheld ethical standards in interactions, fostering 20% trust.	Add trust metric.
Modeled fairness with adherence in tasks, setting high bar.	Tie to bar setting.
Demonstrated accountability in work, inspiring 18% peer standards.	Mention standards inspiration.
Embodied organizational values in operations, enhancing cohesion by 22%.	Insert cohesion metric.
Modeled discipline in interactions, setting consistent example.	Add example setting.
Upheld honesty with 95% consistency in meetings, fostering trust.	Tie to consistency rate.
Exemplified respect in situations, earning 25% confidence.	Add confidence earning.
Consistently embodied professional integrity, strengthening standards.	Mention standards strength.
Modeled ethical standards in tasks, inspiring respect culture.	Tie to culture inspiration.
Demonstrated fairness with morale uplift of 20%, setting example.	Insert uplift metric.
Upheld organizational values in collaborations, fostering 15% trust.	Add trust fostering.

Positive Phrases	Tip
Modeled accountability consistently, enhancing cohesion by 18%.	Tie to cohesion enhancement.
Exemplified honesty in operations, setting conduct standard.	Mention standard setting.
Consistently displayed professional integrity in interactions, inspiring peers.	Add peer inspiration.
Upheld respect with adherence in meetings, fostering 22% confidence.	Insert confidence metric.
Modeled ethical standards in meetings, fostering accountability culture.	Tie to culture fostering.
Integrity in Decisions and Relationships	
Upheld fairness in collaborations, enhancing 20% trust.	Insert trust percentage.
Modeled ethical standards with integrity in decisions, fostering trust.	Add trust fostering.
Demonstrated accountability in relationships, enhancing confidence by 25%.	Tie to confidence metric.
Embodied organizational values with adherence in decisions, inspiring peers.	Mention peer inspiration.
Modeled professional integrity in relationships, setting high standard.	Add standard setting.
Upheld honesty with conduct in decisions, earning 18% respect.	Insert respect earning.
Exemplified respect in relationships, fostering trust culture.	Tie to culture fostering.
Consistently embodied fairness, strengthening 22% cohesion.	Add cohesion metric.
Upheld moral conduct in decisions, enhancing morale by 15%.	Insert morale enhancement.
Modeled discipline with adherence in relationships, inspiring confidence.	Mention confidence inspiration.
Demonstrated ethical standards in decisions, setting positive example.	Add example setting.

Positive Phrases	Tip
Embodied accountability consistently, fostering 20% trust.	Tie to trust fostering.
Modeled organizational values in relationships, enhancing cohesion by 25%.	Insert cohesion percentage.
Upheld professional integrity in decisions, inspiring standards.	Add standards inspiration.
Demonstrated honesty with consistency in relationships, earning 18% confidence.	Tie to confidence earning.
Embodied respect in decisions, fostering respect culture.	Mention culture fostering.
Consistently modeled fairness, strengthening morale.	Add morale strength.
Composure and Professionalism Under Pressure	
Upheld composure in pressure, maintaining professionalism and earning 20% trust.	Insert trust percentage.
Modeled professionalism under pressure, setting high conduct standard.	Add standard setting.
Demonstrated composure in situations, inspiring 25% confidence.	Tie to confidence inspiration.
Embodied resilience under pressure, fostering calm culture.	Mention culture fostering.
Upheld composure consistently, enhancing morale by 18%.	Insert morale metric.
Modeled professional composure in crises, earning respect.	Add respect earning.
Demonstrated integrity under pressure, setting positive example.	Tie to example setting.
Consistently embodied composure, strengthening 22% cohesion.	Add cohesion percentage.
Upheld ethical standards under pressure, inspiring trust culture.	Mention culture inspiration.
Modeled discipline in scenarios, fostering 15% confidence.	Insert confidence fostering.
Demonstrated fairness under pressure, enhancing 20% respect.	Tie to respect enhancement.

BEING A ROLE MODEL

Positive Phrases	Tip
Embodied organizational values under pressure, setting high bar.	Add bar setting.
Modeled honesty with composure in crises, earning 25% trust.	Insert trust earning.
Consistently demonstrated respect under pressure, fostering 18% cohesion.	Add cohesion metric.
Upheld professional integrity under pressure, inspiring standards.	Tie to standards inspiration.
Modeled ethical standards with composure, enhancing morale by 22%.	Insert morale percentage.

Developmental Phrases	Tips
Consistency Between Stated Values and Demonstrated Behavior	
Showed partial alignment in behaviors; recommend journaling to track value consistency daily.	Suggest tracking method.
Demonstrated values inconsistently; suggest peer accountability partners for alignment.	Add partner recommendation.
Aligned actions moderately; advise leadership workshops on behavioral integrity.	Tie to workshop focus.
Exhibited some consistency; recommend self-audits to improve value demonstration.	Insert audit frequency.
Adherence to Professional and Ethical Standards	
Adhered to standards unevenly; suggest ethics training courses for reinforcement.	Add course suggestion.
Maintained adherence basically; recommend case study reviews for ethical dilemmas.	Tie to review type.
Followed standards adequately; advise mentorship on professional conduct.	Mention mentorship source.
Displayed adherence routinely; suggest compliance checklists for daily use.	Insert checklist implementation.
Personal Discipline and Self-management	
Managed self moderately; recommend time-management apps to enhance discipline.	Add app recommendation.
Showed discipline inconsistently; suggest habit-building exercises for consistency.	Tie to exercise type.
Exhibited self-management basically; advise reflection sessions on personal habits.	Insert session frequency.
Maintained discipline adequately; recommend goal-setting frameworks.	Mention framework suggestion.
Visible Demonstration of Desired Team Behaviors	
Demonstrated behaviors partially; suggest role-playing scenarios for practice.	Add scenario practice.
Showed behaviors unevenly; recommend feedback loops from team.	Tie to loop setup.

Developmental Phrases	Tips
Exhibited behaviors routinely; advise visibility training workshops.	Insert workshop details.
Modeled behaviors adequately; suggest behavioral modeling books.	Mention book titles.
Integrity in Decisions and Relationships	
Maintained integrity moderately; recommend integrity-focused seminars.	Add seminar recommendation.
Showed integrity inconsistently; suggest decision-making journals.	Tie to journal use.
Exhibited integrity basically; advise peer discussions on relationships.	Insert discussion frequency.
Demonstrated integrity adequately; recommend ethics case studies.	Mention study type.
Composure and Professionalism Under Pressure	
Managed composure partially; suggest stress management techniques.	Add technique suggestion.
Showed professionalism unevenly; recommend crisis simulation training.	Tie to training type.
Exhibited composure routinely; advise mindfulness practices.	Insert practice recommendation.
Maintained professionalism adequately; suggest composure coaching.	Mention coaching source.
Demonstrated under pressure basically; recommend resilience books.	Add book suggestions.

Needs-Improvement Phrases	Tips
Consistency Between Stated Values and Demonstrated Behavior	
Exhibited inconsistency in value alignment, leading to confusion in team expectations.	Insert confusion impact.
Showed gaps between stated and demonstrated behaviors, affecting 15% morale decline.	Add decline metric.
Aligned actions poorly, resulting in diminished team trust.	Tie to trust diminution.
Demonstrated values sporadically, causing behavioral discrepancies.	Mention discrepancy cause.
Adherence to Professional and Ethical Standards	
Adhered to standards inconsistently, leading to compliance issues.	Insert issue details.
Followed ethical codes poorly, resulting in team skepticism.	Tie to skepticism result.
Maintained adherence minimally, affecting professional reputation.	Add reputation effect.
Displayed standards sporadically, causing ethical lapses.	Mention lapse frequency.
Personal Discipline and Self-management	
Managed self inconsistently, leading to erratic performance.	Insert performance impact.
Showed discipline poorly, resulting in missed deadlines.	Tie to deadline misses.
Exhibited self-management minimally, affecting task completion.	Add completion effect.
Maintained discipline sporadically, causing management gaps.	Mention gap details.
Visible Demonstration of Desired Team Behaviors	
Demonstrated behaviors inconsistently, leading to mixed team signals.	Insert signal impact.
Showed behaviors poorly, resulting in low emulation.	Tie to emulation low.
Exhibited behaviors minimally, affecting team norms.	Add norms effect.

Needs-Improvement Phrases	Tips
Modeled behaviors sporadically, causing behavioral confusion.	Mention confusion cause.
Integrity in Decisions and Relationships	
Maintained integrity inconsistently, leading to relationship strains.	Insert strain details.
Showed integrity poorly, resulting in decision doubts.	Tie to doubt result.
Exhibited integrity minimally, affecting relational trust.	Add trust effect.
Demonstrated integrity sporadically, causing decision inconsistencies.	Mention inconsistency cause.
Composure and Professionalism Under Pressure	
Managed composure inconsistently, leading to pressure mishandlings.	Insert mishandling details.
Showed professionalism poorly, resulting in crisis escalations.	Tie to escalation result.
Exhibited composure minimally, affecting team calm.	Add calm effect.
Maintained professionalism sporadically, causing pressure lapses.	Mention lapse frequency.
Demonstrated under pressure inconsistently, leading to unprofessional reactions.	Insert reaction details.

COLLABORATION

Collaboration assesses a leader's ability to build partnerships, coordinate across boundaries, and align stakeholders around common goals. This trait recognizes that complex problems require collective efforts beyond individual teams or departments.

What Collaboration Measures

- Effectiveness in building cross-functional relationships
- Ability to coordinate efforts across organizational silos
- Success in negotiating mutually beneficial outcomes
- Skill in managing stakeholder expectations and interests
- Capacity to leverage partnerships for enhanced results
- Contribution to organizational integration and collective success

Why Collaboration Matters

Modern organizations operate through networks rather than hierarchies. Leaders rarely control all necessary resources; they must influence peers, negotiate with stakeholders, and coordinate efforts to prevent duplication and create synergies where combined results surpass individual contributions.

Collaboration is essential for complex projects involving diverse expertise, such as product launches (engineering, marketing, sales, operations, finance), military operations (services, agencies, allies), or healthcare delivery (physicians, nurses, administrators, insurers). Leaders who build coalitions effectively guide these efforts.

Practice of Collaboration

Consider a city government sustainability director tasked with reducing carbon emissions by 30% over five years. She coordinates transportation, energy, buildings, waste, and procurement departments by forming a coalition, securing commitments, establishing shared metrics, and facilitating joint sessions. This effort achieves a 28% reduction by year four, Collaboration combines military "Building Coalitions and Collaboration" and Google's "Collaborates across the organization." Both approaches focus on breaking down silos by building relationships, drawing from Amazon's "Invent and Simplify" for integrated innovation and Tesla's partnership-driven approach to reach collective success.

Alternatively, think of a Marine Corps logistics officer managing multinational exercises. He implements planning processes, liaison exchanges, common procedures, and integrated plans that respect national differences. Effective collaboration ensures smooth execution despite the complexities.

Collaboration in Practice

Imagine a city government sustainability director working to reduce municipal carbon emissions by 30% over five years. Success relies on coordinating transportation, energy, buildings, waste management, and procurement, each managed by different departments with competing priorities. She forms a cross-department coalition, secures commitments from each department head, sets shared metrics, and organizes joint problem-solving sessions. Through this coalition, she achieves a 28% reduction by year four, nearing the target through collective effort that no single department could accomplish alone.

Alternatively, imagine an Amry logistics officer coordinating multinational training exercises involving U.S., allied, and partner nation forces. Each country has different equipment, procedures, and command structures. He establishes collaborative planning processes, conducts liaison exchanges to build relationships, develops common operating procedures respecting each nation's requirements, and creates integrated logistics plans. The exercise succeeds because effective coalition-building overcomes inherent complexity.

Connection to Chapter 2 Foundations

Collaboration blends military "Building Coalitions and Collaboration" and Google's "Collaborates across the organization." Both frameworks focus on overcoming silos through relationships, drawing from Amazon's "Invent and Simplify" for integrated innovation and Tesla's partnership-driven approach to achieve collective success.

Positive Phrases	Tips
Effectiveness in Building Cross-functional Relationships	
Built strong cross-functional ties with engineering and marketing, facilitating seamless product launches and 20% faster time-to-market.	Insert time metric.
Forged productive relationships across finance and operations, enabling budget optimizations that saved 15% in costs.	Add cost savings.
Established collaborative bonds with HR and IT departments, enhancing talent acquisition processes by 25%.	Tie to process enhancement.
Developed interdepartmental connections during deployments, improving unit coordination and readiness by 18%.	Mention readiness boost.
Cultivated relationships with supply chain partners, streamlining logistics for 22% efficiency gains.	Insert efficiency percentage.
Nurtured cross-functional alliances in R&D, accelerating innovation cycles by 20%.	Add cycle acceleration.
Strengthened ties with legal and compliance teams, ensuring 100% regulatory adherence in projects.	Tie to adherence rate.
Built effective relationships across sales and customer service, boosting client satisfaction scores by 15%.	Mention score boost.

COLLABORATION

Positive Phrases	Tips
Forged partnerships with external vendors, integrating solutions that reduced downtime by 25%.	Insert downtime reduction.
Established strong inter-unit bonds in military exercises, enhancing joint operational success.	Add success enhancement.
Developed collaborative networks with nonprofit allies, expanding program reach by 30%.	Tie to reach expansion.
Cultivated relationships across healthcare disciplines, improving patient care coordination by 20%.	Mention coordination improvement.
Strengthened cross-functional links in finance, facilitating accurate forecasting with 95% precision.	Insert precision rate.
Built ties with environmental stakeholders, advancing sustainability initiatives by 18%.	Add initiative advancement.
Forged alliances with tech teams, implementing upgrades that increased system uptime to 99%.	Tie to uptime increase.
Nurtured interorganizational relationships, leading to collaborative grants worth $500K.	Mention grant value.
Ability to Coordinate Efforts across Organizational Silos	
Coordinated marketing and sales efforts across silos, achieving 25% revenue growth through unified campaigns.	Insert growth percentage.
Aligned R&D and production teams, breaking silos to deliver products 15% ahead of schedule.	Add schedule advancement.
Facilitated coordination between finance and operations, optimizing resource allocation and saving 20%.	Tie to savings metric.
Bridged silos in military units, coordinating logistics for 95% deployment readiness.	Mention readiness rate.
Harmonized IT and HR efforts, implementing systems that improved employee onboarding by 30%.	Insert onboarding improvement.
Coordinated cross-silo initiatives in healthcare, reducing patient wait times by 18%.	Add time reduction.

Positive Phrases	Tips
Aligned engineering and quality assurance teams, minimizing defects by 25%.	Tie to defect minimization.
Facilitated silo-breaking collaboration in supply chain, enhancing delivery accuracy to 98%.	Mention accuracy enhancement.
Coordinated efforts across legal and compliance silos, achieving zero audit findings.	Add findings status.
Bridged departmental silos in nonprofit projects, increasing impact metrics by 20%.	Insert impact increase.
Harmonized sales and customer service, boosting retention rates by 15%.	Tie to retention boost.
Aligned finance and marketing silos, optimizing ad spend for 22% better ROI.	Add ROI improvement.
Coordinated R&D and regulatory teams, expediting approvals by 25%.	Mention approval expedition.
Facilitated coordination in environmental programs, achieving 18% emission reductions.	Insert reduction percentage.
Bridged silos in tech upgrades, ensuring seamless integration and 20% efficiency gains.	Tie to gain metric.
Harmonized inter-unit efforts in exercises, leading to successful joint operations.	Add operation success.
Success in Negotiating Mutually Beneficial Outcomes	
Negotiated vendor contracts for mutual benefits, securing 20% cost reductions while ensuring quality.	Insert reduction percentage.
Achieved win-win agreements with partners, expanding market access by 25%.	Add access expansion.
Negotiated cross-team resource sharing, resulting in 15% project acceleration.	Tie to acceleration metric.
Secured beneficial alliances in deployments, enhancing mission success by 18%.	Mention success enhancement.
Bargained for collaborative terms in R&D, leading to joint patents and innovations.	Add innovation lead.

COLLABORATION

Positive Phrases	Tips
Negotiated stakeholder compromises, aligning interests for 22% efficiency improvements.	Insert improvement percentage.
Achieved mutually advantageous deals with suppliers, reducing lead times by 20%.	Tie to time reduction.
Negotiated interdepartmental agreements, fostering synergy and 25% productivity gains.	Add gain metric.
Secured win-win outcomes in nonprofit partnerships, increasing funding by 30%.	Mention funding increase.
Bargained for beneficial terms in healthcare collaborations, improving service delivery by 15%.	Insert delivery improvement.
Negotiated finance and operations pacts, optimizing budgets with 18% savings.	Tie to savings percentage.
Achieved mutual benefits in environmental negotiations, advancing goals by 20%.	Add goal advancement.
Secured agreements with tech vendors, enhancing capabilities with 22% cost efficiency.	Mention efficiency enhancement.
Negotiated joint exercise terms, ensuring effective multinational coordination.	Tie to coordination effectiveness.
Bargained for collaborative R&D funds, leading to breakthrough developments.	Add development lead.
Achieved win-win stakeholder deals, aligning for collective success.	Insert success alignment.
Skill in Managing Stakeholder Expectations and Interests	
Managed stakeholder expectations effectively, delivering projects with 95% satisfaction rates.	Insert satisfaction rate.
Balanced diverse interests in cross-functional teams, achieving consensus and 20% faster decisions.	Add decision speed.
Handled expectations in deployments, maintaining alliance cohesion and mission focus.	Tie to cohesion maintenance.
Aligned stakeholder interests in product launches, resulting in successful market entries.	Mention entry success.
Managed interests across silos, fostering buy-in and 15% efficiency boosts.	Insert boost percentage.

Positive Phrases	Tips
Balanced expectations in negotiations, securing commitments for long-term partnerships.	Add partnership security.
Handled diverse stakeholder needs in R&D, accelerating innovations by 25%.	Tie to innovation acceleration.
Managed expectations in supply chain, ensuring timely deliveries with 98% accuracy.	Mention accuracy assurance.
Aligned interests in nonprofit initiatives, increasing volunteer engagement by 20%.	Insert engagement increase.
Balanced stakeholder views in healthcare, improving protocol adherence by 18%.	Add adherence improvement.
Handled finance stakeholder expectations, optimizing investments for 22% returns.	Tie to return optimization.
Managed environmental interests, advancing sustainability with broad support.	Mention support advancement.
Aligned tech stakeholder needs, implementing upgrades with minimal disruptions.	Add disruption minimization.
Balanced interests in joint operations, ensuring smooth executions.	Tie to execution smoothness.
Handled expectations in marketing campaigns, achieving 25% engagement uplift.	Insert uplift metric.
Managed diverse interests, fostering inclusive decision-making.	Add decision fostering.

COLLABORATION

Positive Phrases	Tips
Capacity to Leverage Partnerships for Enhanced Results	
Leveraged vendor partnerships for innovation, resulting in 20% product improvement.	Insert improvement percentage.
Utilized alliances to expand markets, achieving 25% revenue growth.	Add growth metric.
Harnessed cross-functional partnerships, accelerating projects by 15%.	Tie to acceleration percentage.
Leveraged multinational partnerships in deployments, enhancing operational effectiveness.	Mention effectiveness enhancement.
Utilized R&D collaborations, generating breakthrough technologies.	Add technology generation.
Harnessed stakeholder partnerships, optimizing resources for 22% savings.	Insert savings metric.
Leveraged supply chain alliances, improving reliability by 18%.	Tie to reliability improvement.
Utilized nonprofit partnerships, amplifying impact by 30%.	Add impact amplification.
Harnessed healthcare collaborations, enhancing patient outcomes by 20%.	Mention outcome enhancement.
Leveraged finance partnerships, securing investments with favorable terms.	Tie to term security.
Utilized environmental alliances, achieving reduction targets ahead of schedule.	Add schedule achievement.
Harnessed tech partnerships, boosting capabilities by 25%.	Insert capability boost.
Leveraged joint exercise alliances, improving readiness metrics.	Tie to metric improvement.
Utilized marketing collaborations, increasing brand visibility by 15%.	Add visibility increase.
Harnessed interorganizational partnerships, driving collective innovations.	Mention innovation drive.
Leveraged alliances for crisis response, mitigating risks effectively.	Tie to risk mitigation.

Positive Phrases	Tips
Contribution to Organizational Integration & Collective Success	
Contributed to integration initiatives, leading to 20% organizational efficiency gains.	Insert gain percentage.
Advanced collective success through collaborations, achieving enterprise-wide goals.	Add goal achievement.
Promoted integration across silos, resulting in 25% synergy improvements.	Tie to improvement metric.
Contributed to joint success in deployments, enhancing overall mission outcomes.	Mention outcome enhancement.
Advanced organizational unity in R&D, fostering innovative breakthroughs.	Add breakthrough fostering.
Promoted collective efforts, optimizing performance by 18%.	Insert performance optimization.
Contributed to integration in supply chains, reducing costs by 22%.	Tie to cost reduction.
Advanced nonprofit collective success, increasing program efficacy by 30%.	Add efficacy increase.
Promoted healthcare integration, improving care continuity by 15%.	Mention continuity improvement.
Contributed to financial unity, enhancing forecasting accuracy to 95%.	Tie to accuracy enhancement.
Advanced environmental collective goals, achieving sustainability milestones.	Add milestone achievement.
Promoted tech integration, boosting productivity by 20%.	Insert productivity boost.
Contributed to operational success in exercises, improving joint capabilities.	Tie to capability improvement.
Advanced marketing collective efforts, driving 25% campaign success.	Add success drive.
Promoted organizational integration, fostering 18% morale uplift.	Mention uplift metric.
Contributed to enterprise-wide success, aligning for strategic victories.	Tie to victory alignment.

COLLABORATION

Developmental Phrases	Tips
Effectiveness in Building Cross-functional Relationships	
Built relationships adequately; recommend networking events to strengthen cross-functional ties.	Suggest event type.
Developed bonds steadily; suggest joint workshops for better interdepartmental connections.	Add workshop recommendation.
Established ties basically; advise relationship-building training.	Tie to training focus.
Cultivated alliances routinely; recommend stakeholder mapping exercises.	Insert exercise suggestion.
Ability to Coordinate Efforts across Organizational Silos	
Coordinated efforts moderately; suggest silo-breaking team activities.	Add activity recommendation.
Aligned teams adequately; recommend coordination software tools.	Tie to tool suggestion.
Facilitated basically; advise cross-silo meetings for improvement.	Mention meeting frequency.
Bridged silos steadily; suggest integration case studies.	Insert study type.
Success in Negotiating Mutually Beneficial Outcomes	
Negotiated outcomes routinely; recommend negotiation skills courses.	Add course suggestion.
Achieved agreements adequately; suggest win-win strategy workshops.	Tie to workshop focus.
Bargained basically; advise role-playing negotiations.	Mention role-playing.
Secured deals steadily; recommend interest-based bargaining books.	Insert book titles.
Skill in managing stakeholder expectations and interests	
Managed expectations moderately; suggest stakeholder analysis tools.	Add tool recommendation.

Developmental Phrases	Tips
Balanced interests adequately; recommend expectation-setting seminars.	Tie to seminar suggestion.
Handled needs basically; advise feedback collection methods.	Insert method type.
Aligned views steadily; suggest interest alignment frameworks.	Mention framework.
Capacity to Leverage Partnerships for Enhanced Results	
Leveraged partnerships routinely; recommend partnership evaluation metrics.	Add metric suggestion.
Utilized alliances adequately; suggest leverage strategy sessions.	Tie to session recommendation.
Harnessed basically; advise partnership-building retreats.	Mention retreat type.
Leveraged steadily; recommend success case reviews.	Insert review focus.
Contribution to Organizational Integration & Collective Success	
Contributed to integration moderately; suggest unity-building initiatives.	Add initiative recommendation.
Advanced success adequately; recommend collective goal workshops.	Tie to workshop suggestion.
Promoted unity basically; advise integration metrics tracking.	Insert tracking method.
Contributed steadily; suggest success story sharing.	Mention sharing type.
Advanced collective routinely; recommend organizational alignment tools.	Add tool suggestion.

Needs-Improvement Phrases	Tips
Effectiveness in Building Cross-functional Relationships	
Built relationships inadequately, leading to collaboration gaps.	Insert gap details.
Developed bonds poorly, resulting in isolated teams.	Tie to isolation result.
Established ties minimally, affecting interdepartmental support.	Add support effect.
Cultivated alliances sporadically, causing relationship strains.	Mention strain cause.
Ability to Coordinate Efforts across Organizational Silos	
Coordinated efforts inadequately, leading to duplicated work.	Insert work duplication.
Aligned teams poorly, resulting in miscommunications.	Tie to miscommunication result.
Facilitated minimally, affecting project timelines.	Add timeline effect.
Bridged silos sporadically, causing efficiency losses.	Mention loss details.
Success in Negotiating Mutually Beneficial Outcomes	
Negotiated outcomes inadequately, leading to unbalanced deals.	Insert deal imbalance.
Achieved agreements poorly, resulting in lost opportunities.	Tie to opportunity loss.
Bargained minimally, affecting partnership quality.	Add quality effect.
Secured deals sporadically, causing negotiation failures.	Mention failure cause.
Skill in Managing Stakeholder Expectations and Interests	
Managed expectations inadequately, leading to dissatisfaction.	Insert dissatisfaction details.
Balanced interests poorly, resulting in conflicts.	Tie to conflict result.
Handled needs minimally, affecting alignment.	Add alignment effect.

Needs-Improvement Phrases	Tips
Aligned views sporadically, causing expectation mismatches.	Mention mismatch cause.
Capacity to Leverage Partnerships for Enhanced Results	
Leveraged partnerships inadequately, leading to suboptimal results.	Insert result suboptimal.
Utilized alliances poorly, resulting in missed synergies.	Tie to synergy miss.
Harnessed minimally, affecting outcome enhancements.	Add enhancement effect.
Leveraged sporadically, causing partnership underuse.	Mention underuse cause.
Contribution to Organizational Integration & Collective Success	
Contributed to integration inadequately, leading to fragmentation.	Insert fragmentation details.
Advanced success poorly, resulting in isolated achievements.	Tie to achievement isolation.
Promoted unity minimally, affecting collective performance.	Add performance effect.
Contributed sporadically, causing integration lapses.	Mention lapse cause.
Advanced collective inadequately, leading to success shortfalls.	Insert shortfall details.

CONCERN FOR SUBORDINATES

Concern for subordinates evaluates a leader's genuine care for team members' well-being, professional development, and personal circumstances. This trait measures how much leaders view subordinates as valued individuals rather than replaceable resources.

What Concern for Subordinates Measures

- Awareness of and responsiveness to team members' personal and professional needs
- Provision of support during personal or professional challenges
- Advocacy for team members' interests and well-being
- Creation of work environments that respect work-life balance
- Attentiveness to signs of burnout, stress, or disengagement
- Investment in team members' long-term success and satisfaction

Why Concern for Subordinates Matters

Demonstrating genuine concern builds trust, loyalty, and psychological safety, which leads to higher engagement and retention. Team members who feel appreciated as individuals show greater commitment and discretionary effort. They are more likely to raise concerns early, share innovative ideas, and remain with the organization during competitive recruiting.

Concern for Subordinates in Practice

Imagine a retail district manager who notices one of her store managers becoming more stressed and withdrawn. In a private conversation, she learns he's dealing with a family health crisis while balancing full-time responsibilities. She works with him to temporarily adjust his schedule, connects him with company employee assistance programs, and shares some duties with peer managers. The manager manages his personal crisis while maintaining his performance, and his gratitude fosters long-term loyalty and exceptional effort.

Alternatively, consider an Air Force squadron commander who finds out that an enlisted member is facing financial hardship. Instead of dismissing it as a personal matter, the commander connects the member with financial counseling, arranges a temporary interest-free Air Force Relief Society loan, and works with the member's supervisor to explore additional duty pay opportunities. This proactive approach prevents a personal crisis from impacting readiness and demonstrates genuine concern.

Connection to Chapter 2 Foundations

Concern for subordinates directly aligns with the military concept of "Concern for Subordinates" and Google's idea that "Creates an inclusive team environment, showing concern for success and well-being." Both acknowledge that sustainable performance requires leaders to see team members as whole persons, supporting their development and well-being alongside achieving tasks.

CONCERN FOR SUBORDINATES

Positive Phrases	Tip
Awareness of and Responsiveness to Team Members' Personal and Professional Needs	
Demonstrated keen awareness of subordinates' career aspirations, tailoring assignments that led to 20% skill enhancement in key areas.	Insert skill metric.
Responded promptly to personal health concerns, arranging accommodations that maintained 95% productivity during recovery periods.	Add productivity rate.
Showed exceptional responsiveness to professional training needs, securing spots in workshops resulting in 15% performance uplift.	Tie to uplift percentage.
Actively monitored team members' workload stresses, adjusting tasks to prevent overload and improve satisfaction by 25%.	Mention satisfaction boost.
Exhibited strong awareness of cultural needs, implementing inclusive practices that boosted engagement scores by 18%.	Add score improvement.
Responded to feedback on development needs with personalized plans, leading to three promotions within the unit.	Insert promotion count.
Demonstrated empathy for family commitments, offering flexible hours that reduced absenteeism by 20%.	Tie to absenteeism reduction.
Showed attentiveness to skill gaps, providing resources that enhanced team capabilities by 22%.	Add capability enhancement.
Actively addressed professional burnout signs, introducing breaks that sustained high morale during deployments.	Mention morale sustenance.
Responded to personal relocation challenges with support, ensuring seamless transitions and 100% retention.	Tie to retention rate.
Exhibited awareness of mental health needs, facilitating counseling access that decreased stress reports by 15%.	Add report decrease.
Tailored responses to individual learning styles, accelerating professional growth by 25%.	Insert growth acceleration.

Positive Phrases	Tip
Demonstrated responsiveness to work-life conflicts, mediating solutions that improved harmony by 18%.	Tie to harmony improvement.
Showed concern for career plateaus, recommending advancements that led to 20% motivation increase.	Add motivation metric.
Actively listened to personal concerns, implementing changes that fostered trust and 22% loyalty boost.	Mention loyalty boost.
Responded to professional feedback with action, enhancing team proficiency by 15%.	Tie to proficiency enhancement.
Exhibited awareness of diversity needs, creating programs that increased inclusion by 25%.	Add inclusion increase.
Provision of Support During Personal or Professional Challenges	
Provided comprehensive support during a subordinate's illness, coordinating leave that preserved team output at 98%.	Insert output rate.
Offered guidance through professional setbacks, supplying resources that facilitated recovery in two months.	Add recovery time.
Supported team member during family crisis with flexible scheduling, maintaining project deadlines.	Tie to deadline maintenance.
Delivered emotional support in career transitions, providing networking that led to internal opportunities.	Mention opportunity lead.
Assisted subordinates facing financial hardships with referrals, reducing distractions and improving focus by 20%.	Add focus improvement.
Provided mentorship during skill challenges, resulting in 15% competency gains.	Tie to gain percentage.
Offered practical support in relocation, ensuring quick adaptation and 100% operational continuity.	Insert continuity rate.

CONCERN FOR SUBORDINATES

Positive Phrases	Tip
Supported through burnout with mandated rest, restoring performance to peak levels.	Add performance restoration.
Delivered aid during professional conflicts, mediating resolutions that strengthened team dynamics.	Tie to dynamics strength.
Provided resources for personal development challenges, leading to certification achievements.	Mention achievement count.
Offered encouragement in high-pressure deployments, sustaining morale and reducing incidents by 18%.	Add incident reduction.
Supported subordinates' educational pursuits with time off, enhancing qualifications and team expertise.	Tie to expertise enhancement.
Assisted during mental health challenges with confidential help, improving well-being scores by 22%.	Insert score improvement.
Provided logistical support in family emergencies, minimizing absences to under 5%.	Add absence minimization.
Offered career counseling during plateaus, sparking motivation and 20% productivity rise.	Tie to rise percentage.
Delivered support in diversity-related challenges, fostering an inclusive environment.	Mention environment fostering.
Advocacy for Team Members' Interests and Well-being	
Advocated for better wellness benefits, securing programs that reduced health claims by 15%.	Insert claim reduction.
Championed subordinates' interests in promotions, resulting in four advancements within the year.	Add advancement count.
Pushed for equitable workload distribution, improving well-being and retention by 20%.	Tie to retention improvement.
Advocated for mental health days, decreasing burnout cases by 25%.	Mention case decrease.
Defended team interests in resource allocations, enhancing tools and satisfaction by 18%.	Add satisfaction enhancement.

Positive Phrases	Tip
Championed flexible policies for parents, boosting morale by 22%.	Tie to morale boost.
Advocated for diversity training, increasing inclusion metrics by 15%.	Insert metric increase.
Pushed for safety improvements, preventing incidents and improving well-being.	Add prevention detail.
Defended subordinates in performance reviews, ensuring fair assessments and growth.	Tie to growth assurance.
Championed career development funds, leading to skill upgrades for 10 team members.	Mention upgrade count.
Advocated for rest periods in deployments, sustaining health and readiness.	Add readiness sustenance.
Pushed for recognition programs, enhancing well-being and motivation by 20%.	Tie to motivation enhancement.
Defended interests in policy changes, mitigating negative impacts on team.	Insert impact mitigation.
Championed ergonomic upgrades, reducing strain complaints by 25%.	Add complaint reduction.
Advocated for feedback mechanisms, improving well-being through voice.	Tie to voice improvement.
Pushed for professional counseling access, decreasing stress by 18%.	Mention stress decrease.
Creation of Work Environments that Respect Work-life Balance	
Created flexible scheduling environments, reducing overtime by 20% and improving balance.	Insert overtime reduction.
Fostered remote work options, enhancing life satisfaction by 25%.	Add satisfaction enhancement.
Implemented no-email-after-hours policies, boosting recovery and productivity by 15%.	Tie to productivity boost.
Designed team rotations for balance, maintaining readiness during deployments.	Mention readiness maintenance.
Created supportive atmospheres for parents, decreasing turnover by 18%.	Add turnover decrease.
Fostered environments with mandatory breaks, improving focus by 22%.	Tie to focus improvement.

Positive Phrases	Tip
Implemented wellness hours, reducing stress reports by 20%.	Insert report reduction.
Designed inclusive schedules for diverse needs, enhancing engagement by 15%.	Add engagement enhancement.
Created balance-focused cultures, leading to 25% morale uplift.	Tie to uplift metric.
Fostered environments with flexible leaves, improving retention.	Mention retention improvement.
Implemented hobby-sharing sessions, strengthening bonds and balance.	Add bond strengthening.
Designed ergonomic workspaces, reducing fatigue by 18%.	Tie to fatigue reduction.
Created quiet zones for recharge, boosting efficiency by 20%.	Insert efficiency boost.
Fostered vacation encouragement, improving long-term health.	Add health improvement.
Implemented balance training, enhancing awareness and satisfaction by 22%.	Tie to satisfaction enhancement.
Designed family-friendly events, fostering loyalty and balance.	Mention loyalty fostering.
Attentiveness to Signs of Burnout, Stress, or Disengagement	
Monitored burnout signs attentively, intervening with support that reduced cases by 25%.	Insert case reduction.
Showed keen attentiveness to stress, providing relief measures improving morale by 20%.	Add morale improvement.
Detected disengagement early, offering coaching that boosted participation by 15%.	Tie to participation boost.
Attentively addressed burnout in deployments, sustaining performance.	Mention performance sustenance.
Monitored stress indicators, implementing workshops decreasing reports by 18%.	Add report decrease.
Showed attentiveness to disengagement, fostering re-engagement through dialogue.	Tie to re-engagement fostering.
Detected early signs of burnout, providing rest that improved productivity by 22%.	Insert productivity improvement.

Positive Phrases	Tip
Attentively managed stress, connecting to resources reducing absences by 20%.	Add absence reduction.
Monitored disengagement, addressing with incentives boosting motivation.	Tie to motivation boost.
Showed concern for burnout, organizing team-building to alleviate stress.	Mention alleviation detail.
Detected stress proactively, offering mindfulness sessions improving well-being.	Add well-being improvement.
Attentively handled disengagement, providing feedback loops for recovery.	Tie to recovery provision.
Monitored signs attentively, intervening timely to prevent escalations.	Insert prevention detail.
Showed attentiveness to stress, adjusting workloads for balance.	Add balance adjustment.
Detected burnout early, supporting with leaves maintaining team strength.	Tie to strength maintenance.
Attentively addressed disengagement, enhancing involvement through recognition.	Mention involvement enhancement.
Investment in Team Members' Long-term Success and Satisfaction	
Invested in long-term mentoring, leading to 20% career advancement rates.	Insert rate percentage.
Committed to satisfaction through regular surveys, improving scores by 25%.	Add score improvement.
Invested in training programs, enhancing long-term skills and retention by 15%.	Tie to retention enhancement.
Focused on success in deployments, providing education for post-service careers.	Mention career provision.
Committed to satisfaction with wellness investments, reducing turnover by 18%.	Add turnover reduction.
Invested in feedback systems, boosting long-term engagement by 22%.	Tie to engagement boost.
Focused on success through succession planning, preparing for advancements.	Add preparation detail.
Committed to satisfaction with recognition initiatives, improving loyalty by 20%.	Insert loyalty improvement.

CONCERN FOR SUBORDINATES

Positive Phrases	Tip
Invested in professional networks, enhancing career opportunities.	Tie to opportunity enhancement.
Focused on long-term health investments, improving overall well-being.	Add well-being improvement.
Committed to success with personalized development plans, accelerating growth.	Mention growth acceleration.
Invested in satisfaction surveys, addressing issues for 15% uplift.	Tie to uplift metric.
Focused on long-term coaching, leading to skill mastery.	Add mastery lead.
Committed to investments in education, enhancing qualifications.	Tie to qualification enhancement.
Invested in team retreats for bonding, improving long-term cohesion.	Mention cohesion improvement.
Focused on satisfaction through flexible policies, sustaining commitment.	Add commitment sustenance.

Developmental Phrases	Tips
Awareness of and Responsiveness to Team Members' Personal and Professional Needs	
Shows awareness of needs; enhance by regular check-ins for 20% better responsiveness.	Insert check-in frequency.
Maintains steady responsiveness; develop strategic surveys to address satisfaction needs.	Tie to survey use.
Demonstrates good awareness; improve by empathy training for resilient responsiveness.	Add training examples.
Handles needs adequately; strengthen with listening sessions for strategic awareness.	Mention session type.
Provision of Support During Personal or Professional Challenges	
Supports during challenges reliably; refine by resource lists for 15% better aid.	Add list ideas.
Shows good support; develop with crisis protocols for recovery enhancement.	Tie to protocol development.
Maintains support routinely; enhance with peer networks for resilient challenges.	Insert network examples.
Demonstrates solid support; improve by training for strategic challenge management.	Add training types.
Advocacy for Team Members' Interests and Well-being	
Advocates for interests consistently; refine by policy reviews for 18% better well-being.	Mention review ideas.
Shows good advocacy; develop with feedback loops for loyalty enhancement.	Tie to loop use.
Maintains advocacy routinely; enhance with resource advocacy for resilient well-being.	Insert resource examples.
Handles advocacy adequately; boost with meetings for strategic interests.	Add meeting types.
Creation of Work Environments that Respect Work-life Balance	
Creates balance environments reliably; improve by flexibility policies for 20% better harmony.	Mention policy ideas.
Shows good environments; develop with remote options for productivity enhancement.	Tie to option development.

CONCERN FOR SUBORDINATES

Developmental Phrases	Tips
Maintains environments routinely; enhance with surveys for resilient balance.	Insert survey examples.
Demonstrates solid environments; improve by workshops for strategic balance.	Add workshop ideas.
Attentiveness to Signs of Burnout, Stress, or Disengagement	
Attentive to burnout consistently; refine by monitoring tools for 15% better stress detection.	Mention tool ideas.
Shows good attentiveness; develop with wellness checks for prevention enhancement.	Tie to check use.
Maintains attentiveness routinely; enhance with training for resilient stress management.	Insert training examples.
Handles attentiveness adequately; boost with alerts for strategic burnout.	Add alert methods.
Investment in Team Members' Long-term Success and Satisfaction	
Invests in success reliably; improve by career planning for 18% better satisfaction.	Mention planning ideas.
Shows good investment; develop with mentorship for promotion enhancement.	Tie to mentorship use.
Maintains investment routinely; enhance with resources for resilient long-term.	Insert resource examples.
Demonstrates solid investment; improve by reviews for strategic success.	Add review methods.
Handles investment adequately; boost with opportunities for 20% gains.	Mention opportunity types.

Needs-Improvement Phrases	Tips
Awareness of and Responsiveness to Team Members' Personal and Professional Needs	
Falls short in awareness, leading to 15% unmet needs; recommend check-ins.	Insert unmet metric.
Lacks responsiveness, causing satisfaction oversights; pursue surveys.	Tie to oversight impact.
Shows limited awareness, resulting in persistent gaps; develop empathy training.	Add gap details.
Struggles with responsiveness, contributing to 20% low trust; strengthen with sessions.	Mention trust metric.
Provision of Support During Personal or Professional Challenges	
Falls short in support, leading to 18% slow recoveries; recommend resource lists.	Insert recovery metric.
Lacks effective support, causing escalation issues; develop protocols.	Tie to escalation impact.
Shows limited support, resulting in persistent problems; enhance with networks.	Add problem details.
Struggles with challenges, contributing to 15% low aid; boost with training.	Mention aid metric.
Advocacy for Team Members' Interests and Well-being	
Falls short in advocacy, leading to 20% unaddressed well-being; recommend policy reviews.	Insert well-being metric.
Lacks strong advocacy, causing interest gaps; develop feedback loops.	Tie to gap impact.
Shows limited advocacy, resulting in underwell-being; enhance with resource advocacy.	Add underwell-being details.
Struggles with interests, contributing to 18% low well-being; boost with meetings.	Mention well-being metric.
Creation of Work Environments that Respect Work-life Balance	
Falls short in balance, leading to 15% harmony issues; recommend flexibility policies.	Insert harmony metric.
Lacks effective environments, causing imbalance; develop remote options.	Tie to imbalance impact.

Needs-Improvement Phrases	Tips
Shows limited environments, resulting in persistent stress; enhance with surveys.	Add stress details.
Struggles with balance, contributing to 20% low harmony; boost with workshops.	Mention harmony metric.
Attentiveness to Signs of Burnout, Stress, or Disengagement	
Falls short in attentiveness, leading to 18% undetected stress; recommend monitoring tools.	Insert stress metric.
Lacks burnout detection, causing escalations; develop wellness checks.	Tie to escalation impact.
Shows limited attentiveness, resulting in persistent fatigue; enhance with training.	Add fatigue details.
Struggles with stress, contributing to 15% low detection; boost with alerts.	Mention detection metric.
Investment in Team Members' Long-term Success and Satisfaction	
Falls short in investment, leading to 20% stalled success; recommend career planning.	Insert success metric.
Lacks effective investment, causing low satisfaction; develop mentorship.	Tie to satisfaction impact.
Shows limited investment, resulting in undergrowth; enhance with resources.	Add undergrowth details.
Struggles with long-term, contributing to 18% low success; boost with reviews.	Mention success metric.
Demonstrates weak investment, leading to growth gaps; refine with opportunities.	Insert gap details.

COMMUNICATION SKILLS

> *Communication skills assess a leader's ability to convey information, articulate a vision, facilitate dialogue, and ensure shared understanding among diverse audiences. This trait recognizes that effective leadership largely depends on the quality of communication.*

What Communication Skills Measures

- Clarity and conciseness of verbal and written communication
- Ability to adapt communication style to the audience and context
- Effectiveness in articulating vision and strategy
- Active listening and receptiveness to input
- Facilitation of productive dialogue and constructive debate
- Transparency and information-sharing practices

Why Communication Skills Matter

Leaders communicate constantly by setting direction, providing feedback, resolving conflicts, building relationships, managing stakeholders, and inspiring action. Effective communication aligns efforts, prevents misunderstandings, builds trust, and facilitates informed decision-making. However, pitfalls such as withholding information that leads to rumors or relying too heavily on one-way broadcasts without feedback can cause confusion, duplicated effort, missed opportunities, and organizational friction.

Communication effectiveness requires more than just individual eloquence; it ensures that messages are received, understood, and acted upon as intended. A leader who delivers brilliant presentations that team members don't understand fails at communication. Similarly, a leader who listens poorly misses critical input and makes uninformed decisions.

Communication Skills in Practice

Imagine a technology company CEO announcing a major strategic shift from the company's legacy business to emerging opportunities. She carefully crafts tailored messages: investors hear about financial reasons and expected returns; employees learn about career implications and transition support; customers hear commitments to continuity; the board receives detailed risk assessments. Each message addresses specific audience concerns while maintaining a consistent strategic story. This personalized communication helps manage stakeholder anxiety during big changes.

Alternatively, picture a battalion commander preparing his unit for deployment. He holds town halls where families can ask questions, ensures subordinate leaders understand operational plans and the commander's intent, sets up communication protocols for deployed operations, and stays accessible throughout the preparation. This thorough communication builds shared understanding, addresses concerns, and makes sure the information flow supports a successful deployment.

Communication as a Two-Way Process

Effective communication involves both transmitting and receiving information. Leaders must clearly articulate ideas while also actively listening, seeking diverse perspectives, understanding concerns, and incorporating feedback. Leaders who speak well but listen poorly miss important information and risk disengaging team members whose input is ignored.

Connection to Chapter 2 Foundations

Communication skills align with Google's "Is a good communicator, listens and shares information," emphasizing active listening and sharing to foster team alignment. In military systems, it supports traits like "Command Presence," where clear intent and concise directives enable mission success. Amazon's "Earn Trust" principle reinforces attentive listening, honest feedback, and respectful dialogue. Tesla's approach promotes direct communication channels that bypass traditional hierarchies to speed up innovation and problem-solving. These military and corporate frameworks highlight that sustainable leadership depends on high-quality communication that delivers results without harming organizational health.

Positive Phrases	Tip
Clarity and Conciseness of Verbal and Written Communication	
Delivered precise verbal instructions during team briefings, reducing execution errors by 25% in operational tasks.	Insert error reduction.
Crafted concise written memos on policy updates, enabling quick comprehension and 100% compliance across departments.	Add compliance rate.
Articulated project goals with clear verbal directives, accelerating team alignment and completion by 15%.	Tie to completion speed.
Produced succinct reports on financial performance, facilitating executive decisions with zero ambiguities.	Mention decision facilitation.

COMMUNICATION SKILLS

Positive Phrases	Tip
Communicated deployment plans verbally with brevity, enhancing unit readiness by 20%.	Add readiness enhancement.
Wrote clear email summaries of meetings, minimizing follow-up questions by 30%.	Insert question reduction.
Provided concise verbal feedback in reviews, boosting subordinate performance improvements by 18%.	Tie to improvement boost.
Drafted precise strategy documents, streamlining implementation and saving 10% in resources.	Add resource savings.
Delivered clear oral presentations on R&D progress, securing stakeholder buy-in effectively.	Mention buy-in security.
Composed succinct incident reports, enabling rapid response and resolution in crises.	Tie to resolution speed.
Articulated vision in brief town halls, inspiring action and increasing engagement by 22%.	Add engagement increase.
Wrote clear guidelines for processes, reducing training time by 25%.	Insert time reduction.
Communicated changes verbally with conciseness, mitigating resistance and maintaining morale.	Tie to morale maintenance.
Produced precise written analyses, supporting data-driven decisions with high accuracy.	Add accuracy support.
Delivered concise verbal updates in stand-ups, optimizing team coordination by 15%.	Mention coordination optimization.
Crafted clear documentation for software, facilitating user adoption by 20%.	Tie to adoption facilitation.
Ability to Adapt Communication Style to the Audience and Context	
Adapted technical jargon for non-expert stakeholders, ensuring understanding and 95% approval in proposals.	Insert approval rate.

Positive Phrases	Tip
Shifted to motivational style in team huddles, boosting morale by 20% during challenging projects.	Add morale boost.
Tailored formal tone for executive reports, enhancing credibility and decision-making efficiency.	Tie to efficiency enhancement.
Used empathetic style in conflict resolutions, restoring team harmony and productivity by 18%.	Mention productivity restoration.
Adjusted to concise style in deployments, clarifying orders and improving execution by 25%.	Add execution improvement.
Adapted informal style for new hires, accelerating onboarding and integration by 15%.	Tie to integration acceleration.
Shifted to data-driven style for analysts, facilitating insights and 22% better outcomes.	Insert outcome improvement.
Tailored persuasive style for sales pitches, increasing conversions by 20%.	Add conversion increase.
Used adaptive style in cross-cultural meetings, bridging gaps and enhancing collaboration.	Tie to collaboration enhancement.
Adjusted to supportive style in mentoring, fostering growth and 18% skill gains.	Mention gain percentage.
Shifted to urgent style in crises, coordinating responses and minimizing impacts by 25%.	Add impact minimization.
Tailored visual style for presentations, improving retention by 15%.	Tie to retention improvement.
Adapted collaborative style in workshops, generating ideas and 20% innovation uplift.	Insert uplift metric.
Used flexible style in feedback sessions, enhancing receptivity and adjustments.	Tie to adjustment enhancement.
Shifted to strategic style for leaders, aligning visions and strategies effectively.	Add alignment effectiveness.
Tailored audience-specific style in trainings, boosting comprehension by 22%.	Mention comprehension boost.

COMMUNICATION SKILLS

Positive Phrases	Tip
Effectiveness in Articulating Vision and Strategy	
Articulated company vision compellingly, aligning teams and achieving 25% goal attainment increase.	Insert attainment metric.
Conveyed strategic priorities clearly, driving initiatives and 20% efficiency gains.	Add gain percentage.
Expressed long-term vision in addresses, inspiring commitment and 15% engagement rise.	Tie to rise metric.
Outlined strategy in briefings, facilitating execution and success in deployments.	Mention success facilitation.
Articulated innovation strategy, fostering culture and 18% idea generation boost.	Add boost percentage.
Conveyed growth vision to investors, securing funding and expansions.	Tie to funding security.
Expressed ethical strategy in communications, enhancing integrity and trust by 22%.	Insert trust enhancement.
Outlined operational strategy, optimizing processes and reducing costs by 20%.	Add cost reduction.
Articulated team vision in meetings, unifying efforts and improving outcomes.	Tie to outcome improvement.
Conveyed change strategy empathetically, minimizing resistance by 25%.	Mention resistance minimization.
Expressed R&D vision, accelerating developments by 15%.	Add development acceleration.
Outlined safety strategy, achieving zero incidents in high-risk areas.	Tie to incident achievement.
Articulated diversity vision, increasing inclusion metrics by 20%.	Insert metric increase.
Conveyed sustainability strategy, driving eco-initiatives and compliance.	Add compliance drive.
Expressed leadership vision, mentoring successors effectively.	Tie to mentoring effectiveness.
Outlined crisis strategy, coordinating responses and recovery.	Mention recovery coordination.

Positive Phrases	Tip
Active Listening and Receptiveness to Input	
Practiced active listening in sessions, incorporating input and improving plans by 25%.	Insert improvement metric.
Showed receptiveness to feedback, adjusting approaches and boosting satisfaction by 20%.	Add satisfaction boost.
Listened attentively in dialogues, fostering ideas and 15% innovation increase.	Tie to increase metric.
Demonstrated openness to suggestions in deployments, enhancing tactics and success.	Mention success enhancement.
Actively sought input in reviews, refining strategies and outcomes by 18%.	Add outcome refinement.
Showed receptiveness in conflicts, resolving issues and strengthening relationships.	Tie to relationship strength.
Listened to diverse views, integrating perspectives and improving decisions by 22%.	Insert decision improvement.
Demonstrated attentiveness to concerns, addressing them and reducing complaints by 20%.	Add complaint reduction.
Actively encouraged input in brainstorms, generating breakthroughs effectively.	Tie to breakthrough generation.
Showed openness to upward feedback, implementing changes and 25% morale uplift.	Mention uplift metric.
Listened in mentoring, tailoring advice and fostering growth.	Add growth fostering.
Demonstrated receptiveness in surveys, acting on results and improving engagement.	Tie to engagement improvement.
Actively heard stakeholder input, aligning initiatives and satisfaction.	Insert satisfaction alignment.
Showed attentiveness to team ideas, incorporating and boosting ownership by 15%.	Add ownership boost.
Listened during crises, gathering insights and optimizing responses.	Tie to response optimization.

COMMUNICATION SKILLS

Positive Phrases	Tip
Demonstrated openness to peer advice, enhancing collaborations by 20%.	Mention collaboration enhancement.
Facilitation of Productive Dialogue and Constructive Debate	
Facilitated debates in strategy meetings, leading to innovations and 25% better solutions.	Insert solution metric.
Encouraged productive dialogues in teams, resolving conflicts and improving cohesion by 20%.	Add cohesion improvement.
Led constructive debates in workshops, generating ideas and 15% efficiency gains.	Tie to gain metric.
Facilitated dialogues in deployments, clarifying roles and enhancing execution.	Mention execution enhancement.
Encouraged debate in reviews, refining feedback and 18% performance uplift.	Add uplift percentage.
Led productive discussions in cross-teams, fostering synergy and outcomes.	Tie to outcome fostering.
Facilitated constructive exchanges in brainstorms, boosting creativity by 22%.	Insert creativity boost.
Encouraged dialogue in conflicts, achieving resolutions and trust by 20%.	Add trust achievement.
Led debates in planning, optimizing strategies and results.	Tie to result optimization.
Facilitated productive forums, increasing participation by 25%.	Mention participation increase.
Encouraged constructive input in sessions, enhancing decisions.	Add decision enhancement.
Led dialogues in trainings, improving knowledge transfer by 15%.	Tie to transfer improvement.
Facilitated debates in stakeholder meetings, aligning interests effectively.	Mention alignment effectiveness.
Encouraged productive exchanges in retrospectives, driving improvements by 20%.	Add improvement drive.
Led constructive discussions in crises, coordinating actions successfully.	Tie to action coordination.

Positive Phrases	Tip
Facilitated dialogues in diversity initiatives, boosting inclusion by 18%.	Insert inclusion boost.
Transparency and Information-sharing Practices	
Maintained transparent sharing in updates, reducing rumors by 25% and building trust.	Insert rumor reduction.
Practiced open information flow in teams, enhancing alignment by 20%.	Add alignment enhancement.
Shared timely data in reports, facilitating decisions and 15% efficiency.	Tie to efficiency metric.
Ensured transparency in deployments, clarifying info and improving readiness.	Mention readiness improvement.
Practiced sharing in cross-functions, fostering collaboration by 18%.	Add collaboration fostering.
Maintained open practices in feedback, boosting growth by 22%.	Tie to growth boost.
Shared strategic info transparently, aligning visions and outcomes.	Add outcome alignment.
Ensured information flow in projects, minimizing delays by 20%.	Insert delay minimization.
Practiced transparency in budgets, optimizing allocations effectively.	Tie to allocation optimization.
Maintained sharing in trainings, enhancing learning by 25%.	Add learning enhancement.
Shared updates openly, increasing engagement by 15%.	Tie to engagement increase.
Ensured transparent practices in reviews, improving fairness perceptions.	Mention perception improvement.
Practiced information sharing in crises, coordinating responses by 20%.	Add response coordination.
Maintained open flow in stakeholder comms, building partnerships.	Tie to partnership building.
Shared data transparently in R&D, accelerating innovations.	Add innovation acceleration.
Ensured transparency in safety info, achieving compliance by 18%.	Insert compliance achievement.

COMMUNICATION SKILLS

Developmental Phrases	Tip
Clarity and Conciseness of Verbal and Written Communication	
Shows good verbal clarity; enhance by practice sessions for 20% better written conciseness.	Insert session examples.
Maintains steady clarity; develop with editing tools for comprehension improved communication.	Tie to tool use.
Demonstrates solid clarity; improve by feedback on reports for resilient writing.	Add report types.
Handles clarity adequately; strengthen with training for strategic verbal skills.	Mention training examples.
Ability to Adapt Communication Style to the Audience and Context	
Adapts style reliably; refine by audience analysis for 15% better context fit.	Add analysis methods.
Shows good adaptation; develop with cultural training for engagement enhanced style.	Tie to training focus.
Maintains adaptation routinely; enhance with role-playing for resilient audience adjustment.	Insert role-playing examples.
Demonstrates basic adaptation; boost with feedback for strategic style.	Add feedback types.
Effectiveness in Articulating Vision and Strategy	
Articulates vision consistently; improve by storytelling practice for 18% better strategy buy-in.	Mention practice ideas.
Shows good articulation; develop with vision workshops for alignment enhanced articulation.	Tie to workshop focus.
Demonstrates solid vision; enhance with examples for resilient strategy.	Insert example types.
Handles vision adequately; strengthen with training for strategic articulation.	Add training types.
Active Listening and Receptiveness to Input	
Listens actively reliably; refine by note-taking for 20% better receptiveness.	Mention note methods.
Shows good listening; develop with paraphrase practice for ideas enhanced input.	Tie to practice use.
Maintains listening routinely; enhance with questions for resilient receptiveness.	Insert question examples.

Developmental Phrases	Tip
Demonstrates basic listening; boost with training for strategic receptiveness.	Add training ideas.
Facilitation of Productive Dialogue and Constructive Debate	
Facilitates dialogue consistently; improve by agenda setting for 15% better debate.	Mention agenda ideas.
Shows good facilitation; develop with inclusive techniques for innovations enhanced dialogue.	Tie to technique use.
Maintains facilitation routinely; enhance with ground rules for resilient debate.	Insert rule examples.
Handles dialogue adequately; strengthen with training for strategic facilitation.	Add training types.
Transparency and Information-sharing Practices	
Shares information reliably; refine by updates for 18% better transparency.	Mention update ideas.
Shows good sharing; develop with channels for alignment enhanced information.	Tie to channel use.
Maintains sharing routinely; enhance with reports for resilient transparency.	Insert report examples.
Demonstrates solid sharing; improve by training for strategic transparency.	Add training types.
Handles sharing adequately; boost with tools for 20% gains.	Mention tool types.

COMMUNICATION SKILLS

Needs-Improvement Phrases	Tips
Clarity and Conciseness of Verbal and Written Communication	
Falls short in verbal clarity, leading to 20% misunderstandings; recommend practice sessions.	Insert session examples.
Lacks written conciseness, causing errors confusion; pursue editing tools.	Tie to confusion impacts.
Shows limited clarity, resulting in persistent ambiguity; develop feedback on reports.	Add report types.
Struggles with clarity, contributing to 15% low comprehension; strengthen with training.	Mention training examples.
Ability to Adapt Communication Style to the Audience and Context	
Falls short in style adaptation, leading to 18% mismatched messages; recommend audience analysis.	Add analysis methods.
Lacks style flexibility, causing disengagement; develop cultural training.	Tie to disengagement impacts.
Shows limited adaptation, resulting in persistent mismatches; enhance with role-playing.	Insert role-playing examples.
Struggles with audience fit, contributing to 20% low buy-in; boost with feedback.	Add feedback types.
Effectiveness in Articulating Vision and Strategy	
Falls short in vision articulation, leading to 15% misalignment; recommend storytelling practice.	Mention practice ideas.
Lacks strategy clarity, causing execution confusion; develop vision workshops.	Tie to confusion impacts.
Shows limited articulation, resulting in persistent gaps; enhance with examples.	Insert example types.
Struggles with strategy, contributing to 18% low buy-in; strengthen with training.	Add training types.
Active Listening and Receptiveness to Input	
Falls short in active listening, leading to 20% missed input; recommend note-taking.	Mention note methods.

Needs-Improvement Phrases	Tips
Lacks receptiveness, causing overlooked ideas; develop paraphrase practice.	Tie to idea impacts.
Shows limited listening, resulting in persistent disengagement; enhance with questions.	Insert question examples.
Struggles with receptiveness, contributing to 15% low trust; boost with training.	Add training ideas.
Facilitation of Productive Dialogue and Constructive Debate	
Falls short in facilitation, leading to 18% unproductive debates; recommend agenda setting.	Mention agenda ideas.
Lacks effective dialogue, causing silence; develop inclusive techniques.	Tie to silence impacts.
Shows limited facilitation, resulting in persistent conflicts; enhance with ground rules.	Insert rule examples.
Struggles with debate, contributing to 20% low innovation; strengthen with training.	Add training types.
Transparency and Information-sharing Practices	
Falls short in transparency, leading to 15% rumors; recommend updates.	Mention update ideas.
Lacks sharing, causing misalignment; develop channels.	Tie to misalignment impacts.
Shows limited transparency, resulting in persistent confusion; enhance with reports.	Insert report examples.
Struggles with information, contributing to 18% low alignment; boost with training.	Add training types.
Demonstrates weak sharing, leading to trust gaps; refine with tools.	Mention tool types.

EVALUATING SUBORDINATES

Evaluating subordinates assesses a leader's ability to accurately assess team member performance, provide meaningful feedback, fairly document contributions, and make effective personnel recommendations. This trait emphasizes that organizational talent decisions rely on proper evaluation quality.

What Evaluating Subordinates Measures

- Accuracy in assessing individual performance and potential
- Objectivity and fairness in evaluations across diverse team members
- Quality and specificity of performance documentation
- Effectiveness in delivering developmental feedback
- Timeliness and consistency of evaluation processes
- Sound recommendations for promotions, assignments, and development

Why Evaluating Subordinates Matters

Organizations make critical decisions, promotions, assignments, compensation, development investments, retention, based on performance evaluations. Accurate assessments ensure the right people advance to positions of greater responsibility. Inaccurate evaluations, whether inflated ratings that hide performance differences or unfairly harsh judgments, undermine talent decisions and organizational effectiveness.

Fair, developmental evaluations also enhance individual performance. Specific feedback that highlights strengths and areas for development provides actionable guidance. Recognizing contributions boosts motivation. Candid discussions of shortcomings enable course corrections before performance issues become career-limiting.

Evaluating Subordinates in Practice

Consider a consulting firm principal conducting annual reviews for her six-person team. Instead of assigning generic ratings, she documents specific examples: one analyst's exceptional client relationship management, another's analytical depth but communication gaps, and a third's technical mastery with limited business acumen. Her evaluations provide clear differentiation ("Provided objective, differentiated assessments supporting targeted development and promotions"), supporting promotion decisions and targeted development plans. High performers receive recognition supporting advancement; developing performers receive actionable guidance for improvement.

Alternatively, consider a Navy Officer developing annual reviews for junior officers. She maintains detailed performance notes throughout evaluation periods, ensuring assessments reflect comprehensive observation rather than recent events (recency bias). Her evaluations compare each officer against the standard for their rank, not against each other, providing an objective assessment ("Maintained detailed performance notes to counter recency bias, ensuring fair and comprehensive evaluations"). Senior reviewing officers recognize her evaluations as exceptionally accurate, increasing trust in her personnel recommendations.

Evaluation Pitfalls to Avoid

Common evaluation flaws include grade inflation (giving everyone an "excellent" rating), recency bias (favoring recent events), halo effects (letting one strength or weakness dominate the overall assessment), similarity bias (preferring those who are similar to the evaluator), and avoiding difficult conversations (raising ratings to prevent conflict). Effective evaluators identify and address these issues through structured processes, detailed documentation, and a commitment to honest assessment.

Connection to Chapter 2 Foundations

Evaluating subordinates directly aligns with the military's "Evaluating Subordinates" trait, which emphasizes objective assessments to guide personnel decisions and development. Google's "Supports career development and discusses performance" reinforces this through accurate feedback that fosters growth discussions. Amazon's Leadership Principles, such as "Earn Trust" and "Dive Deep," are incorporated into performance reviews by assessing adherence to fair, detailed standards that promote accountability and objectivity. Tesla's annual review process concentrates on the results achieved and the manner in which they were delivered, emphasizing skills evaluation to ensure high performers progress without bias. Together, these frameworks demonstrate that evaluation quality is essential for sustainable talent management and organizational success.

Positive Phrases	Tip
Accuracy in Assessing Individual Performance and Potential	
Delivered precise performance evaluations for 12 team members, incorporating detailed examples of achievements and growth areas that informed targeted development plans.	Insert team member count.
Provided objective feedback sessions that differentiated individual contributions, leading to 5 promotions within the unit based on accurate potential assessments.	Add promotion number.
Maintained comprehensive performance documentation throughout the year, enabling fair comparisons against organizational standards for identifying high-potential talent.	Tie to documentation period.
Conducted timely mid-year reviews for all subordinates, identifying strengths and development needs with actionable plans that enhanced overall team capabilities.	Mention review timing.
Offered balanced assessments that avoided recency bias, drawing from year-long observations to support retention decisions for key personnel.	Add bias avoidance.
Excelled in delivering constructive feedback, resulting in 20% improvement in team performance metrics over six months through accurate evaluations.	Insert improvement percentage.
Demonstrated fairness in evaluating diverse team members, ensuring equitable recognition across backgrounds and roles while spotting untapped potential.	Tie to diversity factors.
Prepared detailed appraisal reports with specific metrics, facilitating informed recommendations for professional development and succession planning.	Add metric examples.
Consistently provided high-quality evaluations that aligned individual goals with organizational objectives, accurately assessing long-term potential.	Mention goal alignment.

EVALUATING SUBORDINATES

Positive Phrases	Tip
Led evaluation processes that fostered open dialogue, enhancing subordinate motivation and engagement through precise performance insights.	Insert dialogue techniques.
Accurately assessed potential in subordinates, recommending 8 for advanced training programs that aligned with strategic needs.	Add recommendation count.
Avoided halo effects by separating assessments of different competencies, providing nuanced feedback that revealed hidden potentials.	Tie to competency separation.
Documented performance with evidence-based examples, supporting defensible promotion boards and accurate talent mapping.	Mention evidence types.
Delivered evaluations on schedule, maintaining consistency across 15 reports without compromising quality in assessing performance trends.	Insert report number.
Promoted fairness by calibrating ratings with peers, ensuring no grade inflation in team assessments while identifying true high-potentials.	Add calibration method.
Provided specific, actionable feedback that led to measurable skill improvements in underperforming team members, accurately gauging recovery potential.	Tie to skill improvements.
Objectivity and Fairness in Evaluations across Team Members	
Conducted thorough reviews that integrated 360-degree input, enhancing evaluation comprehensiveness and fairness across multicultural teams.	Add input sources.
Made sound personnel recommendations based on objective data, aligning with organizational talent needs while ensuring diverse representation.	Tie to recommendation alignment.
Fostered a culture of continuous feedback, conducting quarterly check-ins for 10 subordinates to maintain objectivity.	Insert check-in frequency.

Positive Phrases	Tip
Delivered unbiased evaluations that highlighted both strengths and areas for growth, supporting career progression for diverse staff.	Add balanced examples.
Maintained detailed performance logs to counter similarity bias, ensuring equitable assessments for all team backgrounds.	Tie to bias countering.
Provided timely and specific documentation that informed key assignment decisions with fair considerations for diversity.	Mention decision types.
Excelled in communicating evaluation results clearly, enabling subordinates to own their development in an inclusive manner.	Add communication methods.
Assessed performance against clear criteria, recommending 6 for leadership roles with objective fairness.	Insert recommendation count.
Avoided common pitfalls like leniency bias through structured evaluation frameworks that promoted equity.	Tie to framework use.
Delivered high-fidelity appraisals that drove 15% increase in team productivity through targeted, fair coaching.	Add productivity increase.
Ensured all evaluations included developmental recommendations, promoting long-term growth across diverse profiles.	Mention recommendation types.
Conducted fair and consistent reviews across a multicultural team, enhancing inclusivity and objective insights.	Add team diversity.
Provided evidence-based feedback that supported successful appeals and adjustments with unbiased fairness.	Tie to appeal support.
Excelled at differentiating performance levels, aiding in merit-based rewards while maintaining diversity equity.	Mention reward systems.
Maintained timeliness in all 20 evaluations, with zero delays impacting operations and ensuring fair processes.	Insert evaluation number.

Positive Phrases	Tip
Delivered balanced narratives that captured full performance context, avoiding oversimplification for diverse members.	Add context examples.
Quality and Specificity of Performance Documentation	
Promoted accountability through specific, metric-driven feedback sessions that detailed individual contributions.	Insert metric examples.
Assessed subordinates' potential accurately, leading to optimized team assignments with detailed documentation.	Tie to assignment optimization.
Countered recency effects by referencing historical data in all appraisals for high-quality records.	Add data sources.
Provided comprehensive reports that facilitated executive-level talent discussions with specific examples.	Mention discussion facilitation.
Excelled in fostering trust through transparent and fair evaluation practices documented thoroughly.	Add practice examples.
Delivered developmental feedback that resulted in certifications for 4 team members, with specific notes.	Insert certification count.
Maintained objectivity across high-stakes evaluations, supporting mission-critical decisions with quality docs.	Tie to decision support.
Conducted reviews with precision, incorporating quantitative and qualitative data for specific documentation.	Add data types.
Avoided bias by using standardized rubrics for all 12 subordinates, ensuring high-quality records.	Insert subordinate number.
Provided timely interventions through ongoing performance dialogues documented specifically.	Mention intervention examples.
Excelled at documenting achievements fairly, enhancing organizational equity with detailed narratives.	Tie to equity enhancement.

Positive Phrases	Tip
Made recommendations that aligned talent with strategic priorities, backed by specific documentation.	Add priority alignment.
Delivered evaluations that empowered subordinates with clear growth paths documented in detail.	Mention path examples.
Countered halo bias by evaluating competencies independently with quality, specific notes.	Tie to competency evaluation.
Maintained consistent quality in feedback, driving 20% reduction in performance gaps through documentation.	Add reduction percentage.
Provided nuanced assessments that informed personalized development plans with specific details.	Tie to plan informing.
Effectiveness in Delivering Developmental Feedback	
Excelled in timely delivery of appraisals, ensuring no disruptions to promotion cycles with effective feedback.	Mention cycle impact.
Fostered inclusivity through unbiased recognition of diverse contributions in developmental sessions.	Add contribution examples.
Delivered specific feedback that accelerated career advancements for high potentials effectively.	Tie to advancement acceleration.
Avoided grade inflation by anchoring ratings to observable behaviors in developmental discussions.	Mention behavior anchoring.
Provided thorough documentation supporting legal and operational defensibility in feedback.	Tie to defensibility support.
Excelled at integrating feedback from multiple sources for holistic, effective developmental views.	Add source integration.
Maintained objectivity in cross-functional team evaluations under pressure with effective feedback.	Mention functional examples.
Delivered actionable recommendations that enhanced team capabilities through developmental focus.	Tie to capability enhancement.

Positive Phrases	Tip
Countered biases with calibration sessions, ensuring consistent, effective feedback.	Add session details.
Provided specific, metric-based feedback for sustained development effectiveness.	Mention metric use.
Excelled in recommending assignments that matched skills to needs with developmental intent.	Tie to matching recommendation.
Delivered evaluations with precision, minimizing errors in developmental assessments.	Add error minimization.
Fostered growth mindsets through developmental evaluation approaches effectively.	Mention approach examples.
Avoided leniency by enforcing rigorous evidence requirements in feedback.	Tie to requirement enforcement.
Provided balanced views that supported equitable compensation adjustments developmentally.	Add adjustment support.
Excelled at timely feedback loops, accelerating performance improvements effectively.	Mention improvement acceleration.
Timeliness and Consistency of Evaluation Processes	
Maintained transparent information sharing in evaluations, reducing misunderstandings by 15%.	Insert misunderstanding reduction.
Built trust via consistent, honest evaluation updates to all subordinates.	Add update frequency.
Produced engaging review summaries that kept teams informed and motivated.	Tie to summary content.
Delivered feedback with constructive precision, supporting growth consistently.	Mention growth support.
Maintained consistent messaging across evaluation channels, reinforcing fairness.	Add channel examples.
Ensured shared understanding of performance through targeted review meetings.	Tie to meeting attendance.
Conveyed development values through storytelling in evaluations, resonating with staff.	Mention value examples.
Articulated performance expectations clearly, reducing confusion by 20%.	Add confusion reduction.

Positive Phrases	Tip
Delivered motivational feedback that unified teams around improvement objectives.	Tie to objective unity.
Maintained accessibility through regular evaluation office hours, encouraging dialogue.	Insert hour frequency.
Crafted policy-aligned evaluations with concise language, ensuring adoption.	Add policy examples.
Integrated aids effectively in feedback to simplify complex assessments.	Mention aid types.
Responded to inquiries with prompt, accurate evaluation information, building credibility.	Tie to response time.
Incorporated diverse viewpoints in evaluations, enhancing buy-in.	Add viewpoint sources.
Led evaluation training, elevating dialogue quality consistently.	Mention training results.
Articulated risks clearly in assessments, enabling informed decisions.	Add risk examples.
Sound Recommendations for Promotions, Assignments, and Development	
Fostered transparency in promotion discussions, minimizing misalignment.	Tie to misalignment minimization.
Excelled in jargon-free language for staff, improving comprehension in recommendations.	Add comprehension improvement.
Delivered feedback with precision, supporting growth in assignments.	Mention growth examples.
Maintained consistent messaging, reinforcing alignment in development.	Add messaging channels.
Facilitated sessions valuing voices, leading to sound recommendations.	Tie to session outcomes.
Conveyed appreciation effectively, enhancing retention in promotions.	Add retention improvements.
Handled challenges with adaptive strategies in assignments.	Mention strategy examples.
Led communications minimizing resistance through rationale in development.	Add resistance metrics.
Demonstrated etiquette in calls, enhancing satisfaction in recommendations.	Tie to satisfaction improvements.

EVALUATING SUBORDINATES

Positive Phrases	Tip
Facilitated reviews with balanced dialogue for sound assignments.	Add balance achieved.
Articulated paths clearly in sessions, motivating talent for promotions.	Mention path descriptions.
Maintained channels for feedback, incorporating into recommendations.	Add channel examples.
Excelled in delivery, engaging with Q&A in development sessions.	Tie to engagement metrics.
Conveyed protocols with clarity, ensuring compliance in assignments.	Add compliance evidence.
Built relationships through correspondence for sound promotions.	Mention relationship gains.
Promoted transfer via documentation in development recommendations.	Add documentation types.
Handled escalations with focus in assignment communications.	Tie to solution examples.

Developmental Phrases	Tips
Accuracy in Assessing individual Performance and Potential	
Shows good assessment accuracy; enhance by incorporating data tools for 20% better potential identification.	Insert tool examples.
Maintains steady accuracy; develop with bias training to refine promotion performance judgments.	Tie to training focus.
Demonstrates solid accuracy; improve by peer calibration for resilient assessments.	Add calibration methods.
Handles accuracy adequately; strengthen with historical reviews for strategic potential.	Mention review examples.
Objectivity and Fairness in Evaluations Across Team Members	
Exhibits objectivity reliably; refine by diversity training for 15% fairer diverse evaluations.	Add training ideas.
Shows good fairness; develop with rubrics to boost inclusivity equitable ratings.	Tie to rubric use.
Maintains fairness routinely; enhance with feedback for resilient objectivity.	Insert feedback examples.
Demonstrates basic objectivity; improve by audits for strategic fairness.	Add audit types.
Quality and Specificity of Performance Documentation	
Documents performance consistently; refine by templates for 18% better specificity.	Mention template ideas.
Shows good documentation; develop with evidence logs for defensibility enhanced quality.	Tie to log use.
Maintains documentation routinely; enhance with tools for resilient records.	Insert tool examples.
Handles documentation adequately; boost with training for strategic quality.	Add training types.

Developmental Phrases	Tips
Effectiveness in Delivering Developmental Feedback	
Delivers feedback reliably; improve by coaching sessions for 20% better developmental impact.	Mention session ideas.
Shows good effectiveness; develop with examples for growth enhanced feedback.	Tie to example use.
Maintains effectiveness routinely; enhance with follow-ups for resilient development.	Insert follow-up examples.
Demonstrates solid effectiveness; strengthen with training for strategic feedback.	Add training ideas.
Timeliness and Consistency of Evaluation Processes	
Ensures timeliness consistently; refine by schedules for 15% better consistency.	Mention schedule ideas.
Shows good timeliness; develop with reminders for delays enhanced processes.	Tie to reminder use.
Maintains consistency routinely; enhance with calendars for resilient timeliness.	Insert calendar examples.
Handles timeliness adequately; boost with tools for strategic consistency.	Add tool types.
Sound Recommendations for Promotions, Assignments, and Development	
Makes recommendations reliably; improve by data analysis for 18% better soundness.	Mention analysis ideas.
Shows good recommendations; develop with reviews for assignments enhanced personnel.	Tie to review use.
Maintains recommendations routinely; enhance with consultations for resilient soundness.	Insert consultation examples.
Demonstrates solid recommendations; strengthen with training for strategic personnel.	Add training types.
Handles recommendations adequately; boost with metrics for 20% gains.	Mention metric types.

Needs-Improvement Phrases	Tips
Accuracy in Assessing Individual Performance and Potential	
Falls short in assessment accuracy, leading to 15% misjudged potential; recommend data tools.	Insert tool examples.
Lacks precise judgments, causing promotions poor assessments; pursue bias training.	Tie to assessment impacts.
Shows limited accuracy, resulting in persistent errors; develop peer calibration.	Add error details.
Struggles with potential, contributing to 20% low judgments; strengthen with reviews.	Mention judgment metric.
Objectivity and Fairness in Evaluations Across Team Members	
Falls short in objectivity, leading to 18% unfair ratings; recommend diversity training.	Add training ideas.
Lacks fairness, causing bias issues; develop rubrics.	Tie to bias impacts.
Shows limited objectivity, resulting in persistent inequities; enhance with feedback.	Insert inequity details.
Struggles with fairness, contributing to 15% low equity; boost with audits.	Add equity metric.
Quality and Specificity of Performance Documentation	
Falls short in documentation quality, leading to 20% vague records; recommend templates.	Mention template ideas.
Lacks specific documentation, causing defensibility gaps; develop evidence logs.	Tie to gap impacts.
Shows limited quality, resulting in persistent oversights; enhance with tools.	Add oversight details.
Struggles with specificity, contributing to 18% low quality; strengthen with training.	Mention quality metric.

EVALUATING SUBORDINATES

Needs-Improvement Phrases	Tips
Effectiveness in Delivering Developmental Feedback	
Falls short in feedback effectiveness, leading to 15% stalled development; recommend coaching sessions.	Add session ideas.
Lacks impactful feedback, causing weak growth; develop with examples.	Tie to growth impacts.
Shows limited effectiveness, resulting in persistent underdevelopment; enhance with follow-ups.	Insert underdevelopment details.
Struggles with developmental, contributing to 20% low impact; boost with training.	Add impact metric.
Timeliness and Consistency of Evaluation Processes	
Falls short in timeliness, leading to 18% delayed processes; recommend schedules.	Mention schedule ideas.
Lacks consistency, causing disruptions; develop reminders.	Tie to disruption impacts.
Shows limited timeliness, resulting in persistent delays; enhance with calendars.	Add delay details.
Struggles with consistency, contributing to 15% low reliability; strengthen with tools.	Mention reliability metric.
Sound Recommendations for Promotions, Assignments, and Development	
Falls short in sound recommendations, leading to 20% mismatched personnel; recommend data analysis.	Add analysis ideas.
Lacks effective recommendations, causing poor alignments; develop with reviews.	Tie to alignment impacts.
Shows limited soundness, resulting in persistent mismatches; enhance with consultations.	Add mismatch details.
Struggles with recommendations, contributing to 18% low effectiveness; strengthen with training.	Mention effectiveness metric.
Demonstrates weak recommendations, leading to gaps; refine with metrics.	Add gap details.

CATEGORY 3

CHARACTER

> *Character encompasses the personal qualities that earn trust, inspire confidence, and sustain performance during adversity.*

While Results measures outputs and Leadership assesses interpersonal effectiveness, Character evaluates the inner qualities that define a leader's core. People with exceptional character motivate others to achieve extraordinary things through personal examples. Leaders with character flaws, dishonesty, selfishness, or lack of courage eventually lose the trust, confidence, and respect of their subordinates, discovering they cannot sustain organizational success alone. This category, rooted in the military's emphasis on moral courage and resilience, includes two traits that reflect integrity and perseverance under pressure:

- Initiative
- Resilience

INITIATIVE

*Initiative assesses a leader's proactive behavior,
such as taking action without specific instructions,
anticipating needs, recognizing opportunities,
and advancing progress independently. This trait
distinguishes proactive leaders from reactive
ones, who wait for direction, by highlighting how
proactive leaders generate opportunities through
their own initiative.*

What Initiative Measures

- Proactive identification of problems and opportunities
- Independent action to address issues without awaiting direction
- Anticipation of future needs and preemptive preparation
- Drive to improve processes and outcomes beyond minimum requirements
- Ownership mindset and accountability for results
- Energy and forward momentum in pursuing objectives

Why Initiative Matters

Organizations constantly face evolving challenges that demand flexible responses. Leaders who demonstrate initiative identify emerging issues before they escalate into crises, capitalize on opportunities ahead of others, and maintain momentum when guidance is uncertain. Initiative-driven leaders lessen supervisory burdens, eliminate the need for constant instructions, and promote organizational agility through proactive problem-solving. However, risks such as overstepping authority or taking unnecessary chances can cause poor decisions and disruptions. Initiative is especially crucial in uncertain situations where formal guidance lags behind actual conditions. A leader with initiative assesses the situation, works within their authority, and takes sensible risks instead of waiting for perfect clarity that may never arrive.

Initiative in Practice

Consider a hospital operations manager who notices that patient discharge processes cause delays affecting bed availability. Without being instructed to do so, she analyzes discharge workflows, identifies bottlenecks in pharmacy and transportation coordination, proposes integrated scheduling changes, pilots improvements on two floors, documents 35% faster discharge times, and presents her findings recommending hospital-wide implementation ("Identified operational bottlenecks proactively, piloting improvements that achieved 35% efficiency gains"). This self-initiated improvement project demonstrates initiative that drives operational excellence.

Alternatively, a Marine Corps logistics officer preparing for deployment might identify potential supply chain vulnerabilities based on recent intelligence about host-nation port capacity. Without waiting for higher headquarters' directions, he develops contingency plans for alternative supply routes, pre-positions additional logistics assets, and coordinates with allied nations for backup facilities. "Anticipated supply vulnerabilities and developed contingencies independently, ensuring operational continuity during restrictions." When port access becomes limited during deployment, his initiative prevents supply shortfalls that could have compromised operations.

Balancing Initiative with Authority

Initiative doesn't mean acting without coordination or exceeding authority. Effective initiative works within proper boundaries by identifying opportunities and taking actions within one's scope of control, while appropriately raising issues that require higher-level decisions. A leader who takes initiative within these limits demonstrates good judgment; a leader who acts unilaterally beyond authority shows poor judgment despite their energetic effort.

Connection to Chapter 2 Foundations

The initiative directly reflects the military's "Initiative" trait, which values self-starting actions to advance mission goals in dynamic environments. Google's "Is productive and results-oriented" supports this by highlighting self-motivation to achieve results without constant supervision. Amazon's "Ownership" principle encourages leaders to take initiative for the company's benefit, thinking long-term and acting beyond their immediate roles without waiting for instructions. Tesla's performance culture promotes initiative by carefully assessing innovative, self-driven contributions that speed up results in a fast-paced setting. Collectively, these frameworks show that proactive leadership builds sustainable momentum and organizational resilience.

Positive Phrases	Tip
Proactive Identification of Problems and Opportunities	
Proactively identified emerging supply chain vulnerabilities, developing detailed contingency plans that prevented major disruptions during peak operational seasons.	Insert specific disruption details.
Anticipated team training needs well ahead of deployment schedules, independently organizing targeted workshops that enhanced operational readiness by 25%.	Add exact readiness percentage.
Took ownership of process inefficiencies without any direction, redesigning workflows that achieved 20% faster project completion in high-stakes R&D environments.	Tie to precise completion speed.
Independently pursued professional development opportunities, applying new skills to drive a 15% improvement in key team performance metrics across departments.	Mention the improvement metric.

Positive Phrases	Tip
Foreseeing resource shortages in advance, preemptively secured additional assets, ensuring seamless execution of critical missions in demanding military operations.	Add details on asset security.
Demonstrated forward momentum by initiating cross-departmental collaborations that expanded project scope successfully by 30% in collaborative settings.	Insert scope expansion details.
Without awaiting instructions, analyzed market trends and launched initiatives that captured 18% of new business opportunities in competitive landscapes.	Tie to opportunity capture rate.
Proactively addressed safety concerns in daily operations, implementing new protocols that reduced incidents by 22% over the fiscal year.	Add incident reduction percentage.
Took independent action to mentor junior staff members, fostering a culture of continuous improvement and innovation in dynamic corporate settings.	Mention culture fostering aspects.
Anticipated regulatory changes on the horizon, preparing compliance strategies that maintained uninterrupted business operations during key transitions.	Tie to operation maintenance.
Drove proactive problem-solving in ambiguous situations, resolving issues before they escalated into crises during high-pressure product launches.	Add crisis prevention details.
Independently identified cost-saving opportunities, optimizing budgets to achieve 25% savings without compromising quality in resource management.	Insert savings percentage achieved.
Foreseeing team morale dips during challenges, initiated wellness programs that boosted productivity by 20% across the organization.	Tie to productivity boost metric.
Took ownership of innovation projects from start, developing prototypes that led to patented solutions and market advantages in tech industries.	Add specific patent details.

Positive Phrases	Tip
Proactively networked with industry partners, securing collaborations that enhanced organizational capabilities by 15% in strategic alliances.	Mention capability enhancement.
Without direction, streamlined administrative processes, reducing processing time by 18% and improving efficiency overall.	Tie to time reduction achieved.
Anticipated technological needs proactively, implementing upgrades that improved system reliability by 22% in critical infrastructure.	Add reliability improvement.
Independent Action to Address Issues without Direction	
Independently researched best practices in the field, applying them to elevate team standards and exceed quarterly goals by 25%.	Insert goal exceedance percentage.
Drove momentum in stalled projects by taking decisive action, completing deliverables ahead of schedule in fast-paced corporate environments.	Add schedule advancement details.
Foreseeing competitive threats early, developed counter-strategies that maintained market share growth of 20% despite challenges.	Tie to growth maintenance rate.
Proactively volunteered for high-visibility assignments, delivering results that advanced organizational objectives by 15%.	Mention objective advancement.
Took independent steps to enhance diversity initiatives, resulting in an 18% more inclusive workforce through targeted efforts.	Add inclusivity increase percentage.
Anticipated environmental risks in operations, implementing sustainable practices that cut waste by 22% annually.	Tie to waste cut reduction.
Without awaiting approval, piloted efficiency trials that scaled to organization-wide improvements saving 25% in costs.	Insert saving metric details.
Drove proactive engagement with stakeholders, resolving potential conflicts before they arose in complex military contexts.	Add conflict resolution aspects.

Positive Phrases	Tip
Independently optimized supply inventories, preventing shortages and saving 20% in procurement costs over the period.	Tie to cost saving achieved.
Foreseeing skill gaps in the team, organized targeted training sessions that upskilled members by 15% in key areas.	Add upskill percentage metric.
Took ownership of quality control issues, introducing measures that improved product standards by 18% consistently.	Mention standard improvement.
Proactively sought feedback loops from peers, refining processes to achieve 22% better customer satisfaction ratings.	Tie to satisfaction improvement.
Anticipated operational bottlenecks ahead, reallocating resources to maintain 25% on-time delivery rates effectively.	Add delivery maintenance percentage.
Drove innovation without supervision, launching apps that streamlined internal communications by 20% for the team.	Insert streamlining percentage.
Independently addressed compliance gaps, ensuring zero audit findings in annual reviews through thorough checks.	Tie to finding status achieved.
Foreseeing market shifts proactively, adjusted strategies, resulting in 15% revenue growth for the quarter.	Add growth result percentage.
Took decisive action in crises, mitigating risks and restoring operations 18% faster than expected timelines.	Tie to restoration speed.
Anticipation of Future Needs and Preemptive Preparation	
Proactively built resilience plans, preparing the team for unforeseen challenges effectively in volatile markets.	Add challenge preparation details.
Without awaiting orders, revamped training curricula, improving skill acquisition rates by 25% among participants.	Insert rate improvement percentage.
Drove momentum in community outreach efforts, building partnerships that enhanced organizational reputation by 20%.	Tie to reputation enhancement.

INITIATIVE

Positive Phrases	Tip
Anticipated logistical challenges in advance, pre-positioning assets to ensure mission success in deployments.	Add asset pre-positioning details.
Independently optimized supply inventories, preventing shortages and saving 15% in procurement costs annually.	Mention saving percentage.
Foreseeing skill gaps proactively, organized targeted training sessions that upskilled the team by 18% overall.	Tie to upskill metric achieved.
Took ownership of quality control issues, introducing measures that improved product standards significantly in manufacturing processes.	Add standard significance details.
Proactively sought feedback loops, refining processes to achieve 22% better customer satisfaction scores.	Insert satisfaction metric.
Anticipated operational bottlenecks, reallocating resources to maintain 25% on-time delivery rates consistently.	Tie to delivery rate maintenance.
Drove innovation without supervision, launching apps that streamlined internal communications by 20% efficiency.	Add streamlining metric.
Independently addressed compliance gaps, ensuring zero audit findings in annual corporate reviews.	Mention finding zero status.
Foreseeing market shifts, adjusted strategies proactively, resulting in 15% revenue growth over the period.	Tie to growth percentage.
Took decisive action in crises, mitigating risks and restoring operations 18% faster than anticipated.	Add speed faster details.
Proactively built resilience plans, preparing the team for unforeseen challenges with effective strategies.	Tie to plan effectiveness.
Without awaiting orders, revamped training curricula, improving skill acquisition rates by 22% through updates.	Insert acquisition improvement.
Drove momentum in community outreach, building partnerships that enhanced reputation across stakeholders.	Add partnership building.

Positive Phrases	Tip
Anticipated logistical challenges, pre-positioning assets to ensure success in high-stakes operations.	Tie to success assurance.
Drive to Improve Processes and Outcomes Beyond Minimum Requirements	
Independently optimized supply inventories, preventing shortages and saving 25% in costs through smart planning.	Insert cost saving percentage.
Foreseeing skill gaps, organized training sessions that upskilled the team by 20% in essential competencies.	Add upskill percentage.
Took ownership of quality issues, introducing measures that improved standards by 15% across production.	Tie to standard improvement.
Proactively sought feedback, refining processes for 18% better satisfaction among clients and teams.	Insert satisfaction better metric.
Anticipated bottlenecks, reallocating resources for 22% on-time delivery improvement in logistics.	Add delivery percentage.
Drove innovation, launching apps that streamlined communications by 25% in internal workflows.	Tie to streamlining percentage.
Independently addressed gaps, ensuring zero findings in audits through comprehensive reviews.	Add finding zero status.
Foreseeing shifts, adjusted strategies for 20% growth in market presence and revenue.	Insert growth metric.
Took action in crises, restoring operations 15% faster than standard recovery times.	Tie to faster restoration.
Proactively built plans, preparing the team thoroughly for potential challenges ahead.	Add preparation for details.
Revamped curricula, improving acquisition rates by 18% with updated content and methods.	Insert rate improvement.
Drove outreach, enhancing reputation by 22% through strategic community partnerships.	Tie to reputation enhancement.
Anticipated challenges, ensuring success by pre-positioning resources effectively.	Add success ensuring aspects.
Optimized inventories, saving 25% in procurement through proactive adjustments.	Insert saving metric.

Positive Phrases	Tip
Organized sessions, upskilling the team by 20% in targeted professional areas.	Tie to upskilling metric.
Introduced measures, improving standards significantly in quality control processes.	Add measure introduction.
Ownership Mindset and Accountability for Results	
Proactively sought feedback mechanisms, achieving 15% satisfaction increase through process refinements.	Insert achievement metric.
Reallocated resources strategically, maintaining delivery rates during peak demands effectively.	Tie to resource reallocation.
Launched innovative apps, streamlining communications by 18% for better team coordination.	Add app launch details.
Addressed compliance gaps independently, ensuring zero findings in rigorous annual audits.	Tie to gap addressing.
Adjusted strategies proactively, resulting in sustained growth across key performance areas.	Add strategy adjustment.
Mitigated risks decisively, restoring operations faster in crisis response scenarios.	Tie to risk mitigation.
Built comprehensive plans, preparing the team effectively for emerging challenges.	Add plan building details.
Revamped curricula without guidance, improving acquisition rates significantly.	Tie to curricula revamp.
Built strategic partnerships, enhancing reputation through community outreach efforts.	Add partnership built.
Pre-positioned assets anticipatorily, ensuring success in mission-critical deployments.	Tie to asset pre-positioning.
Optimized inventories independently, preventing shortages in supply chain management.	Add inventory optimization.
Organized training sessions, upskilling the team in vital skills for future needs.	Tie to session organization.
Introduced quality measures, improving standards across manufacturing operations.	Add measure introduction.

Positive Phrases	Tip
Sought stakeholder feedback, refining processes for enhanced operational efficiency.	Tie to feedback sought.
Reallocated resources dynamically, maintaining delivery amid fluctuating demands.	Add resource reallocation.
Launched communication apps, streamlining interactions for improved productivity.	Tie to app launch.
Addressed ethical gaps, ensuring full compliance in all organizational reviews.	Add gap addressing.
Energy and Forward Momentum in Pursuing Objectives	
Adjusted strategies dynamically, resulting in 25% growth in revenue and market share.	Insert growth result.
Mitigated risks effectively, restoring operations 20% faster in high-stakes situations.	Add faster restoration.
Built robust plans, preparing the team for challenges with proactive measures.	Tie to plan building.
Revamped curricula independently, improving rates by 15% in skill development.	Insert rate improvement.
Drove outreach initiatives, building partnerships for long-term collaboration.	Add outreach drive.
Anticipated challenges early, pre-positioning assets for seamless execution.	Tie to challenge anticipation.
Optimized inventories proactively, saving costs in procurement and logistics.	Add cost saving details.
Organized sessions strategically, upskilling by 18% in core competencies.	Insert upskilling by.
Introduced innovative measures, improving 22% standards in quality assurance.	Add standard improving.
Sought feedback proactively, achieving better satisfaction through refinements.	Tie to satisfaction achieving.
Reallocated resources efficiently, maintaining 25% delivery in operations.	Insert delivery maintaining.
Launched apps with initiative, streamlining by 20% in communication flows.	Add streamlining by.

INITIATIVE

Positive Phrases	Tip
Addressed gaps thoroughly, ensuring zero findings in compliance checks.	Tie to finding ensuring.
Foreseeing shifts accurately, adjusted for growth in strategic planning.	Add shift foreseeing.
Took bold action, mitigating risks effectively in crisis management.	Tie to action took.
Built team resilience, preparing for unforeseen operational demands.	Add resilience built.

Developmental Phrases	Tips
Proactive Identification of Problems and Opportunities	
Identifies problems adequately; suggest trend analysis training to boost proactive opportunity spotting.	Add training suggestion.
Shows steady identification; develop with market research tools for better anticipation.	Tie to tool development.
Demonstrates good proactive; improve by networking for resilient opportunity ID.	Mention networking improvement.
Handles identification routinely; strengthen with feedback for strategic problems.	Add feedback strength.
Independent Action to Address Issues without Direction	
Takes action reliably; refine by decision frameworks for 20% better independent resolutions.	Insert resolution better.
Shows good independent; develop with risk assessment for enhanced action.	Tie to assessment development.
Maintains action routinely; enhance with simulations for resilient independent.	Add simulation enhancement.
Demonstrates solid action; improve by training for strategic independent.	Mention training improve.
Anticipation of Future Needs and Preemptive Preparation	
Anticipates needs consistently; refine by forecasting tools for 15% better preparation.	Add tool refine.
Shows good anticipation; develop with scenario planning for enhanced needs.	Tie to planning development.
Maintains anticipation routinely; enhance with reviews for resilient preemptive.	Insert review enhancement.
Handles anticipation adequately; boost with workshops for strategic needs.	Add workshop boost.
Drive to Improve Processes and Outcomes Beyond Minimum Requirements	
Drives improvement reliably; improve by benchmark studies for 18% better outcomes.	Mention study improve.

Developmental Phrases	Tips
Shows good drive; develop with innovation labs for enhanced processes.	Tie to lab development.
Maintains drive routinely; enhance with metrics for resilient improvement.	Insert metric enhancement.
Demonstrates solid drive; strengthen with training for strategic outcomes.	Add training strengthen.
Ownership Mindset and Accountability for Results	
Exhibits ownership consistently; refine by accountability frameworks for better mindset.	Add framework refine.
Shows good ownership; develop with goal setting for enhanced accountability.	Tie to setting development.
Maintains ownership routinely; enhance with audits for resilient mindset.	Insert audit enhancement.
Handles ownership adequately; boost with coaching for strategic accountability.	Add coaching boost.
Energy and Forward Momentum in Pursuing Objectives	
Pursues objectives reliably; improve by motivation techniques for 20% better momentum.	Mention technique improve.
Shows good energy; develop with time management for enhanced pursuing.	Tie to management development.
Maintains energy routinely; enhance with challenges for resilient momentum.	Insert challenge enhancement.
Demonstrates solid energy; strengthen with training for strategic objectives.	Add training strengthen.
Handles energy adequately; boost with incentives for better pursuing.	Mention incentive boost.

Needs-Improvement Phrases	Tips
Proactive Identification of Problems and Opportunities	
Falls short in proactive ID, leading to 15% missed opportunities; recommend trend training.	Add training recommend.
Lacks opportunity spotting, causing oversight issues; pursue research tools.	Tie to issue causing.
Shows limited proactive, resulting in persistent problems; develop networking.	Add problem resulting.
Struggles with identification, contributing to 20% low anticipation; strengthen feedback.	Mention anticipation low.
Independent Action to Address Issues without Direction	
Falls short in independent action, leading to 18% delayed resolutions; recommend frameworks.	Add framework recommend.
Lacks decisive action, causing escalation; develop risk assessment.	Tie to escalation causing.
Shows limited independent, resulting in persistent waits; enhance simulations.	Add wait resulting.
Struggles with action, contributing to 15% low resolutions; boost training.	Mention resolution low.
Anticipation of Future Needs and Preemptive Preparation	
Falls short in anticipation, leading to 20% unprepared needs; recommend forecasting tools.	Add tool recommend.
Lacks preemptive, causing gap issues; develop scenario planning.	Tie to gap causing.
Shows limited anticipation, resulting in persistent shortages; enhance reviews.	Add shortage resulting.
Struggles with needs, contributing to 18% low preparation; boost workshops.	Mention preparation low.
Drive to Improve Processes and Outcomes beyond Minimum Requirements	
Falls short in drive, leading to 15% stagnant outcomes; recommend benchmark studies.	Add study recommend.
Lacks improvement, causing minimum adherence; develop innovation labs.	Tie to adherence causing.
Shows limited drive, resulting in persistent basics; enhance metrics.	Add basic resulting.

Needs-Improvement Phrases	Tips
Struggles with processes, contributing to 20% low beyond; strengthen training.	Mention beyond low.
Ownership Mindset and Accountability for Results	
Falls short in ownership, leading to 18% unaccounted results; recommend frameworks.	Add framework recommend.
Lacks mindset, causing responsibility gaps; develop goal setting.	Tie to gap causing.
Shows limited ownership, resulting in persistent lacks; enhance audits.	Add lack resulting.
Struggles with accountability, contributing to 15% low results; boost coaching.	Mention result low.
Energy and Forward Momentum in Pursuing Objectives	
Falls short in energy, leading to 20% stalled momentum; recommend motivation techniques.	Add technique recommend.
Lacks forward, causing pursuit issues; develop time management.	Tie to issue causing.
Shows limited energy, resulting in persistent slows; enhance challenges.	Add slow resulting.
Struggles with momentum, contributing to 18% low pursuing; strengthen training.	Mention pursuing low.
Demonstrates weak energy, leading to objective gaps; refine incentives.	Add gap leading.

RESILIENCE

> *Resilience assesses a leader's ability to stay effective during high-stress situations and recover from setbacks. This combined trait reflects both how well they perform in immediate crises and their longer-term ability to bounce back from adversity.*

What Resilience Measures

- Performance during high-stress, high-stakes situations
- Composure and clear thinking when facing urgent demands
- Decision quality under time pressure and uncertainty
- Recovery from setbacks, failures, or disappointments
- Positive attitude maintenance despite adversity
- Learning and adaptation following difficulties

Why Resilience Matters

Resilience is rooted in the Character category because it reflects internal qualities rather than learned skills. True resilience stems from emotional maturity, perspective, self-awareness, and values that provide stability during difficult times. Leaders with strong character maintain their integrity under pressure, even when compromising values seems easier, demonstrating steadfastness that inspires their teams.

Leadership naturally involves pressure, quick decisions, resource limitations, competing demands, unexpected crises, and major failures. Effective leaders prevent problems from escalating, make wise choices despite uncertainty, and create a steady presence that reassures teams during chaos. However, pitfalls like breaking down under stress or becoming defensive after failures can block learning, worsen situations, and damage confidence.

Resilience extends beyond crisis management to long-term recovery from setbacks. When projects fail, initiatives fall short, or external issues disrupt plans, resilient leaders handle disappointment positively, learn lessons from failures, stay motivated, and model good adaptation that fosters organizational learning. These qualities help evaluators understand how resilient leaders manage challenges.

Resilience in Practice

Consider a cybersecurity director responding to a ransomware attack that encrypts critical systems during peak business hours. Under extreme pressure, with the CEO demanding immediate answers and operations teams unable to function, she stays composed, activates incident response protocols, coordinates technical teams and legal counsel, communicates openly about known facts and response timelines, and makes sequential decisions. "Maintained composure during ransomware crisis, coordinating response to minimize downtime and preserve integrity", balancing recovery speed with forensic integrity. Her ability to remain calm under pressure prevents panic-driven decisions that could worsen the situation.

Alternatively, consider a military company commander whose unit suffers casualties during combat operations. Despite personal grief and the weight of responsibility, he remains focused on operations, ensures proper care for the wounded, consolidates the tactical position, reports the situation accurately to higher command, and maintains unit cohesion ("Demonstrated resilience in combat, processing casualties while ensuring continued operational readiness") during extreme stress. Later, he processes the emotional impact appropriately while staying prepared for future operations. This demonstrates both the ability to perform under immediate pressure and longer-term resilience in managing trauma.

Balancing Resilience with Self-Care

Resilience doesn't mean pushing through endless stress without support. Real resilience involves knowing your limits, seeking resources like counseling or peer support, and encouraging team self-care to avoid burnout. Leaders who balance resilience with self-care maintain long-term effectiveness, demonstrating healthy adaptation instead of stoic isolation.

Connection to Chapter 2 Foundations

Resilience directly corresponds with the military's "Ability Under Pressure/Resilience" trait, exemplified by programs like the Army's Comprehensive Soldier Fitness Program that focus on maintaining performance and adapting to adversity. Google's "Is productive and results-oriented" supports this by suggesting sustained output under stress through effective management. Amazon's "Deliver Results" principle encourages overcoming setbacks with resilience to succeed despite challenges. Tesla's performance evaluations emphasize resilience in high-pressure environments, focusing on learning from failures to spur innovation. Together, these frameworks highlight that resilient leadership promotes organizational stability and growth through adversity.

Positive Phrases	Tip
Performance During High-Stress, High-Stakes Situations	
Delivered exceptional performance in ransomware attack, achieving minimal downtime despite intense pressure from stakeholders.	Insert situation like 'ransomware attack'.
Sustained high-level output during stressful operations, exceeding 20% of expected targets in product launch crises.	Replace 20% with actual figure.
Maintained operational excellence in chaotic high-stakes environments, ensuring continuity during military deployments.	Add combat examples for military.

RESILIENCE

Positive Phrases	Tip
Excelled under extreme stress, delivering 25% faster resolutions in critical financial audits.	Specify scenarios to show prevention.
Performed reliably in high-pressure stakes, optimizing budget amid resource limits in R&D projects.	Insert budget limits for Amazon-style.
Upheld peak standards during intense situations, contributing to 15% mission success in emergency responses.	Customize with situation types.
Executed tasks flawlessly under high stakes, yielding efficiency gains in uncertain market shifts.	Add disruption details for uncertainty.
Demonstrated steadfast performance in stressful high-stakes deployments, maintaining team effectiveness under fire.	Insert deployment examples.
Delivered consistent results amid high-pressure demands, achieving 18% efficiency in corporate restructurings.	Specify demands like CEO inquiries.
Sustained focus and output in extreme situations, preventing 22% escalation of supply chain issues.	Add issue examples to emphasize.
Performed at elite levels during high-stakes crises, securing organizational stability in economic downturns.	Link to failures like launches.
Maintained superior performance under stress, driving 25% better outcomes in healthcare operations.	Tie to operations like launches.
Excelled in high-stakes environments, ensuring adherence despite competing demands in legal compliances.	Insert demands to stress quick-decision.
Delivered unwavering performance during intense periods, boosting 20% team readiness in training exercises.	Customize with periods like peaks.
Upheld high standards in stressful situations, achieving targets despite unexpected challenges in sales quotas.	Add challenge examples for adversity.
Performed effectively under high stakes, yielding 15% improved resilience in project teams.	Specify team impacts for inspiration.

Positive Phrases	Tip
Composure and Clear Thinking when Facing Urgent Demands	
Exhibited calm composure amid urgent demands, enabling clear strategies and successful crisis resolution.	Insert demands like answers.
Maintained clear thinking during high-urgency scenarios, coordinating responses with precision in attacks.	Add scenarios like attacks.
Demonstrated poised composure under pressing demands, fostering rational team actions in disruptions.	Specify demands to emphasize.
Retained clarity in thought amid urgent pressures, minimizing errors and achieving uptime in halts.	Customize disruptions for handling.
Showed unflappable composure facing immediate demands, guiding teams through chaos in failures.	Add chaos examples to highlight.
Maintained composed clarity during urgent escalations, ensuring thoughtful decisions in uncertainties.	Insert escalations for management.
Exhibited steady thinking under demanding urgencies, stabilizing operations and metrics in reports.	Specify urgencies like reports.
Demonstrated clear-headed composure amid high-urgency crises, preventing panic and boosting confidence.	Add crises to stress reassurance.
Retained poised clarity facing urgent operational demands, optimizing recovery speed in downturns.	Insert demands to tie to preservation.
Maintained composure and sharp thinking during pressing situations, driving positive outcomes in combat.	Customize situations like failures.
Showed calm resolve under urgent pressures, facilitating coordinated responses in emergencies.	Add pressure examples for maturity.
Exhibited clear thinking in high-urgency environments, achieving better coordination in deployments.	Tie to environments like combat.

Positive Phrases	Tip
Demonstrated composed clarity amid demanding urgencies, inspiring team cohesion in traumas.	Insert urgencies for stability.
Retained steady composure facing urgent disruptions, ensuring continuity in shifts.	Customize disruptions for response.
Maintained clear perspective under pressing demands, yielding strategic advantages in audits.	Add demands to emphasize choices.
Showed unflinching composure during urgent crises, enhancing decision effectiveness in attacks.	Link to crises for Google's focus.
Decision Quality Under Pressure and Uncertainty	
Made high-quality decisions swiftly under time pressure, mitigating 20% risks effectively in crises.	Insert pressures like timelines.
Delivered sound judgments amid uncertainty, achieving targets despite ambiguous conditions in launches.	Customize uncertainties like flaws.
Exercised wise decision-making under tight time constraints, preventing worsening issues in audits.	Add constraint examples for management.
Rendered quality choices in uncertain high-pressure scenarios, optimizing outcomes in attacks.	Specify scenarios like attacks.
Made prudent decisions swiftly amid ambiguities, ensuring 25% operational integrity in downturns.	Tie to ambiguities for balance.
Demonstrated decisive quality under time-sensitive uncertainties, driving recoveries in failures.	Insert uncertainties for adaptation.
Delivered balanced judgments in pressured uncertain environments, boosting success in combat.	Customize environments like combat.
Exercised clear decision-making amid time pressures, yielding strategic gains in emergencies.	Add pressures to highlight choices.

Positive Phrases	Tip
Made effective choices under uncertain timelines, preventing escalation and achieving efficiency.	Specify timelines for decision.
Rendered high-quality decisions in ambiguous pressures, fostering team stability in traumas.	Add ambiguity examples for reassurance.
Demonstrated sound judgment under time-constrained uncertainties, enhancing resilience in deployments.	Tie to uncertainties for Amazon.
Made wise sequential decisions amid pressures, balancing speed and accuracy in halts.	Customize pressures to stress integrity.
Delivered quality verdicts in uncertain high-time scenarios, driving positive turns in failures.	Insert scenarios for success link.
Exercised prudent choices under pressing ambiguities, securing long-term growth in markets.	Add ambiguities for learning.
Made reliable decisions swiftly amid uncertainties, yielding improved readiness in exercises.	Customize uncertainties for Fitness.
Rendered balanced high-quality decisions under time pressures, inspiring confidence in teams.	Add pressure examples for steadfastness.
Recovery from Setbacks, Failures, or Disappointments	
Recovered resiliently from product failure, restoring revenue within six months through focused efforts.	Insert setbacks like 'product failure'.
Bounced back effectively from disappointments, achieving 30% turnaround in performance metrics.	Customize disappointments for turnaround.
Overcame major failures with fortitude, transforming losses into eventual successes through revisions.	Add failure examples to tie to mortems.
Rebounded positively from setbacks, maintaining 25% momentum and cohesion in teams.	Specify setbacks like casualties.

Positive Phrases	Tip
Navigated disappointments resiliently, yielding full recovery and enhancements in operations.	Insert disappointments for handling.
Recovered from operational failures, implementing 20% preventive measures successfully.	Customize failures to highlight lessons.
Overcame team and personal setbacks, fostering renewed motivation and output.	Add setbacks for confidence rebuilding.
Bounced back from project disappointments, delivering 15% revised achievements.	Insert project types to tie to feedback.
Recovered steadfastly from high-impact failures, driving growth post-event in innovations.	Customize impacts for Tesla link.
Handled setbacks with resilient grace, restoring confidence and 18% output.	Add grace examples to emphasize motivation.
Rebounded effectively from external disruptions, achieving strategic realignments.	Tie to disruptions for Amazon overcoming.
Overcame disappointments through positive recovery, yielding better trajectories in goals.	Customize disappointments for stability.
Recovered from failures with unwavering resolve, ensuring sustained excellence in tasks.	Insert failures to stress maturity.
Bounced back resiliently from setbacks, optimizing future preparedness by 22%.	Add setbacks for adaptation.
Navigated major disappointments, transforming them into opportunities for advancement.	Customize disappointments for recovery.
Recovered effectively from high-stakes failures, boosting team resilience by 25%.	Add failure examples for impact.
Positive Attitude Maintenance Despite Adversity	
Maintained positive attitude amid crises, inspiring 20% morale uplift in teams.	Insert adversities like crises.
Upheld optimistic demeanor despite setbacks, driving sustained efforts in projects.	Customize setbacks for perseverance.
Preserved constructive mindset in adverse conditions, enhancing team resilience by 15%.	Add condition examples for dynamics.

Positive Phrases	Tip
Kept upbeat outlook amid disappointments, reframing as growth chances in launches.	Specify disappointments for opportunity.
Sustained encouraging attitude under adversity, boosting collaboration by 18%.	Tie to adversities for unity.
Maintained hopeful perspective despite failures, achieving renewed vigor in operations.	Insert failures for motivational.
Upheld affirmative stance in chaotic adversities, stabilizing performance by 22%.	Customize adversities for confidence.
Preserved resilient positivity amid uncertainties, yielding better outcomes in markets.	Add uncertainties to highlight reassurance.
Kept motivational attitude despite pressing adversities, preventing morale dips by 25%.	Specify adversities for steadiness.
Maintained optimistic resolve under adverse pressures, inspiring adaptability in teams.	Add pressure examples for Google's.
Upheld positive energy amid major disappointments, fostering unity by 20%.	Insert disappointments for rebuilding.
Preserved constructive outlook despite high-stakes adversities, driving progress.	Add adversities for inspiration.
Maintained encouraging demeanor in failure-laden conditions, boosting motivation by 15%.	Customize conditions for reframing.
Kept hopeful attitude amid disruptions, achieving sustained readiness in deployments.	Add disruptions for alignment.
Upheld affirmative perspective despite setbacks, yielding enhanced cohesion by 18%.	Specify setbacks for stability.
Preserved resilient optimism in adverse scenarios, inspiring long-term growth by 22%.	Add scenario examples for navigation.
Learning and Adaptation Following Difficulties	
Learned key insights from post-mortems, adapting for 25% efficiency improvements in processes.	Insert difficulties like 'post-mortems'.
Adapted effectively post-setback, incorporating lessons to enhance future performance by 20%.	Customize setbacks for Fitness.

RESILIENCE

Positive Phrases	Tip
Drew valuable lessons from failures, implementing adaptive changes successfully for innovations.	Add failure examples for Tesla.
Evolved strategies after difficulties, fostering organizational growth by 15%.	Specify difficulties for measures.
Integrated insights from adversities, adapting to achieve better preparedness by 18%.	Tie to adversities for revisions.
Transformed challenges into adaptive learning, yielding innovative successes in launches.	Insert challenges for modeling.
Learned and pivoted post-disappointments, optimizing processes resiliently by 22%.	Customize disappointments for redevelopment.
Adapted resiliently following pressures, enhancing leadership effectiveness by 25%.	Add pressures for perspective.
Drew lessons from crises, implementing adaptive enhancements for teams.	Specify crises for fostering.
Evolved approaches after setbacks, modeling adaptive behavior by 20%.	Add setback examples for learning.
Integrated failure insights for adaptations, driving recoveries in operations.	Tie to failures for overcoming.
Learned proactively from difficulties, ensuring long-term adaptability by 15%.	Customize difficulties for emphasis.
Adapted strategies post-adversities, yielding improved resilience in units.	Insert adversities for self-awareness.
Drew adaptive lessons from uncertainties, achieving strategic evolutions by 18%.	Add uncertainties for adjustments.
Evolved resiliently following disappointments, fostering organizational learning by 22%.	Customize disappointments for motivational.
Learned from high-stakes difficulties, implementing forward-thinking changes by 25%.	Add difficulty examples for stability.
Integrated post-difficulty insights, adapting for sustained excellence in tasks.	Tie to insights for values-based.

Developmental Phrases	Tips
Performance During High-stress, High-stakes Situations	
Maintained basic performance in ransomware attack, but output dipped 15%; recommend stress management training.	Insert situation and training.
Sustained operations during stress, yet missed targets; suggest prioritizing key tasks under pressure.	Replace with specific goal.
Handled high-stakes demands adequately, but efficiency fell 20%; advise simulation exercises for improvement.	Add military examples.
Performed steadily in intense situations, though resource use suboptimal; recommend efficiency workshops.	Specify situations.
Composure and Clear Thinking when Facing Urgent Demands	
Showed partial composure amid urgent demands, but clarity wavered; suggest mindfulness practices for focus.	Insert demands.
Maintained thinking during urgencies, yet hesitated in chaos; recommend role-playing for composure.	Add scenarios.
Demonstrated some poise under pressures, but reactions inconsistent; advise feedback sessions on rationality.	Specify demands.
Retained basic clarity facing disruptions, but errors increased 18%; suggest peer mentoring for refinement.	Customize disruptions.
Decision Quality Under Pressure and Uncertainty	
Made acceptable decisions under time pressure, but risks rose 15%; recommend decision-framework training.	Insert pressures.
Delivered judgments amid uncertainty, yet overlooked options; suggest scenario planning exercises.	Customize uncertainties.
Exercised basic wisdom in constraints, but issues worsened; advise review processes for prevention.	Add constraint examples.

RESILIENCE

Developmental Phrases	Tips
Rendered choices in high-pressure scenarios, though integrity lapsed; recommend ethics workshops.	Specify scenarios.
Recovery from Setbacks, Failures, or Disappointments	
Recovered gradually from product failure, but timeframe extended; suggest post-event debriefs for bounce-back.	Insert setbacks.
Bounced back from disappointments, yet momentum lagged 20%; recommend motivation strategies.	Customize disappointments.
Overcame failures partially, but losses persisted; advise lesson-logging for transformation.	Add failure examples.
Rebounded from setbacks, though cohesion dipped; suggest team-building for positivity.	Specify setbacks.
Positive Attitude Maintenance Despite Adversity	
Maintained moderate positivity amid crises, but morale uplift limited 15%; recommend optimism coaching.	Insert adversities.
Upheld demeanor despite setbacks, yet efforts flagged; suggest reframing techniques for perseverance.	Customize setbacks.
Preserved mindset in conditions, but resilience varied 18%; advise support networks for dynamics.	Add condition examples.
Kept outlook amid disappointments, though growth slow; recommend journaling for opportunity.	Specify disappointments.
Learning and Adaptation Following Difficulties	
Learned some insights from difficulties, but adaptations partial 20%; suggest structured reviews.	Insert difficulties.
Adaptation lagged post-setback, ignoring lessons; recommend feedback loops for enhancement.	Customize setbacks.

Developmental Phrases	Tips
Lessons ignored from failures, resulting in stalled changes; advise innovation workshops for success.	Add failure examples.
Evolved after difficulties, though growth limited; suggest mentorship for measures.	Specify difficulties.
Integrated insights from adversities, but preparedness lagged; recommend planning sessions.	Tie to adversities.

RESILIENCE

Needs-Improvement Phrases	Tip
Performance During High-stress, High-stakes Situations	
Performance declined in ransomware attack, resulting in shortfalls and 20% delays.	Insert situation.
Output faltered during stressful operations, missing 15% of targets due to mishandling.	Replace with figure.
Failed to maintain excellence in chaotic environments, causing disruptions and strain.	Add combat examples.
Underperformed in intense situations, leading to suboptimal 18% efficiency and escalations.	Specify situations.
Composure and Clear Thinking when Facing Urgent Demands	
Lost composure amid urgent demands, leading to unclear strategies and setbacks.	Insert demands.
Thinking clouded during high-urgency scenarios, resulting in imprecise responses and errors.	Add scenarios.
Lacked poise under pressing demands, fostering irrational actions and 20% downtime.	Specify demands.
Clarity diminished facing disruptions, increasing 15% operational errors.	Customize disruptions.
Decision Quality Under Pressure and Uncertainty	
Decisions suffered under time pressure, escalating 18% risks and issues.	Insert pressures.
Judgments erred amid uncertainty, missing due to overlooked ambiguities.	Customize uncertainties.
Decision-making faltered in constraints, worsening 20% problems.	Add constraint examples.
Choices lacked quality in high-pressure scenarios, compromising integrity.	Specify scenarios.

Needs-Improvement Phrases	Tip
Recovery from Setbacks, Failures, or Disappointments	
Recovery stalled from product failure, extending timeframe and losses.	Insert setbacks.
Failed to bounce back effectively from disappointments, causing 15% performance drops.	Customize disappointments.
Overcame failures inadequately, perpetuating losses and declines.	Add failure examples.
Rebound weakened from setbacks, eroding 18% cohesion and momentum.	Specify setbacks.
Positive Attitude Maintenance Despite Adversity	
Attitude turned negative amid crises, contributing to 20% morale decline.	Insert adversities.
Demeanor faltered despite setbacks, hindering sustained efforts.	Customize setbacks.
Mindset eroded in adverse conditions, reducing 15% team resilience.	Add condition examples.
Outlook dimmed amid disappointments, missing growth opportunities.	Specify disappointments.
Learning and Adaptation Following Difficulties	
Gleaned minimal insights from difficulties, leading to 18% repeated inefficiencies.	Insert difficulties.
Adaptation lagged post-setback, ignoring lessons and hindering performance.	Customize setbacks.
Lessons ignored from failures, resulting in 20% stalled changes.	Add failure examples.
Strategies unevolved after difficulties, limiting growth.	Specify difficulties.
Insights unintegrated from adversities, causing 15% preparedness deficits.	Tie to adversities.

CATEGORY 4

INTELLECT

Intellect assesses a leader's mental capabilities, dedication to ongoing learning, and ability to apply knowledge to benefit the organization. This category examines reasoning, judgment, decision-making, and intellectual growth. Unlike innate intelligence, which stays relatively stable, intellectual ability can be enhanced through experience, education, and intentional practice. Assessing intellect offers valuable insights into a leader's capacity to manage complexity, learn from experiences, and make sound decisions under uncertain conditions. Most importantly, it indicates whether a leader has the necessary cognitive foundation for greater responsibilities. This category includes three key traits.

- Judgement
- Decision Making
- Professional Education

JUDGMENT

> *Judgment assesses a leader's ability to evaluate situations accurately, consider options wisely, understand the consequences of decisions, and arrive at solid conclusions. This trait reflects the quality of thinking that comes before action.*

What Judgment Measures

- Accuracy in assessing situations and understanding context
- Wisdom in weighing alternatives and considering consequences
- Recognition of second-order effects and unintended outcomes
- Application of experience and professional knowledge to situations
- Discernment in distinguishing critical from peripheral issues
- Prudence in managing risk and uncertainty

Why Judgment Matters

Technical skills, hard work, and good intentions cannot substitute for good judgment. A leader with flawed judgment makes decisions that cause problems, misallocate resources, misread situations, and lead to unintended consequences. However, pitfalls such as overemphasizing immediate pressures (which can lead to quick fixes) or failing to anticipate second-order effects can trigger a chain reaction of issues. Conversely, strong judgment enables leaders to handle ambiguity, avoid predictable problems, identify the best actions, and make sensible decisions when perfect information is unavailable. Judgment develops through experience, reflection, and learning from mistakes. Junior leaders with limited experience often rely heavily on procedures, guidance, and consultation. Senior leaders with sound judgment can operate effectively in new situations by applying principles learned from diverse experiences.

Judgment in Practice

Consider a hospital emergency department director facing a bed capacity crisis during a flu season surge. Sound judgment is needed to balance competing concerns: patient safety (not turning away emergencies), staff well-being (who are already working long hours), operational constraints (physical bed limits), regulatory requirements (staffing ratios), and financial implications (overtime costs). Good judgment leads her to implement surge protocols, coordinate with regional hospitals for overflow capacity, authorize temporary staffing increases, and set clear criteria for transferring less-acute patients, managing the crisis without compromising safety or overworking staff.

Alternatively, consider a battalion commander evaluating intelligence about potential enemy activity. The intelligence is ambiguous, with indicators suggesting a possible threat but lacking confirmation. Sound judgment weighs probabilities, potential consequences of action versus inaction, resource costs of heightened posture, and mission priorities. He decides to increase defensive measures in proportion to the threat level while continuing to gather intelligence. "Weighed ambiguous intelligence effectively, implementing proportionate measures to mitigate threats," demonstrating prudent risk management amid uncertainty.

For comparison, poor judgment occurs when a manufacturing supervisor handling quality issues decides to ship marginal products to meet quarterly goals, reasoning that most customers won't notice and complaints can be addressed later. This mistake leads to warranty costs, damage to customer relationships, and potential safety liabilities, and outcomes far worse than the short-term benefit of meeting targets. Flawed judgment often involves overvaluing immediate pressures while underestimating long-term consequences.

Balancing Judgment with Consultation

Judgment isn't just about making decisions alone. Good judgment involves considering different perspectives and consulting others when necessary, especially in complex or high-stakes situations, to reduce personal biases and improve decision quality. Leaders who combine independent thinking with input show maturity, avoid overconfidence, and benefit from collective wisdom.

Connection to Chapter 2 Foundations

Judgment directly correlates with the military's "Judgment" trait, highlighting weighing pros and cons to make appropriate decisions, and "Intellect and Wisdom" for applying experience in uncertain situations. Google's "Is a strong decision maker" provides the cognitive foundation for making well-considered actions under uncertainty. Amazon's "Have Backbone; Disagree and Commit" and "Dive Deep" principles reinforce judgment through respectful challenges and thorough analysis to reach sound conclusions. Tesla emphasizes data-driven judgment when evaluating results and decision quality in innovative, high-pressure environments. Together, these frameworks show that superior judgment fosters effective leadership across various fields, ensuring sustainable success.

Positive Phrases	Tip
Accuracy in Assessing Situations and Understanding Context	
Assessed situations with exceptional accuracy, identifying key context factors that drove effective responses in volatile markets.	Insert specific situations.
Demonstrated precise understanding of complex contexts, enabling informed assessments in ambiguous deployment environments.	Tailor to organizational contexts.
Evaluated scenarios thoroughly, capturing nuanced details that enhanced overall situational awareness during product launches.	Replace with details like stakeholder dynamics.
Provided accurate assessments of team dynamics, fostering proactive adjustments to maintain performance in R&D teams.	Customize to team or project specifics.
Identified critical context elements swiftly, contributing to 20% reduction in misaligned decisions during crises.	Insert actual percentage.
Maintained high accuracy in situational reviews, minimizing errors in high-stakes financial evaluations.	Adapt to stakes like financial risks.
Excelled in contextual analysis, revealing hidden factors that influenced strategic outcomes in military operations.	Provide examples of factors.
Delivered spot-on assessments of operational contexts, supporting seamless adaptations in supply chain disruptions.	Tailor to operations like supply chain.
Showed keen insight into situational nuances, achieving efficiency improvements in cross-functional projects.	Replace with specific value like efficiency.
Accurately gauged environmental factors, enabling 25% better alignment with objectives in competitive landscapes.	Customize to environmental types.
Exhibited flawless accuracy in assessing risks, preventing potential pitfalls in regulatory changes.	Insert risk examples.

Positive Phrases	Tip
Understood contextual implications deeply, driving 18% enhancement in team coordination during transitions.	Adapt to coordination scenarios.
Provided reliable situational assessments, contributing to successful navigation of uncertainties in market volatility.	Tailor to uncertainty types.
Demonstrated superior accuracy in evaluating contexts, yielding cost savings in resource allocations.	Replace with specifics like cost savings.
Identified key situational drivers with precision, optimizing resource allocation in economic trends.	Provide drivers examples.
Maintained consistent accuracy in assessments, supporting 22% decision success rate in high-pressure scenarios.	Insert actual percentage.
Wisdom in Weighing Alternatives & Considering Consequences	
Weighed alternatives with exceptional wisdom, considering long-term consequences effectively in strategic planning.	Insert alternatives like strategic options.
Balanced pros and cons prudently, minimizing unintended impacts in decision processes during budget overruns.	Tailor to impacts like team morale.
Evaluated options thoughtfully, ensuring alignment with organizational values and goals in ethical dilemmas.	Replace with values like ethical standards.
Demonstrated sage consideration of consequences, avoiding short-sighted choices in investment decisions.	Customize to choices like investments.
Weighed risks and benefits astutely, achieving 15% better outcomes in process improvements.	Insert actual percentage.
Applied wisdom in alternative analysis, fostering sustainable solutions in environmental initiatives.	Adapt to solutions like process improvements.
Considered multifaceted consequences, enhancing decision quality by reducing inefficiencies.	Replace with specific value like efficiency.

Positive Phrases	Tip
Balanced competing interests wisely, mitigating potential downsides in stakeholder negotiations.	Provide interests examples.
Exhibited prudent evaluation of alternatives, supporting strategic success in expansions.	Tailor to strategic contexts.
Weighed implications with foresight, reducing 20% negative effects in operational disruptions.	Customize to effects like disruptions.
Demonstrated insightful consequence assessment, optimizing resource use in budget spending.	Insert resource types.
Evaluated trade-offs effectively, ensuring positive long-term results in cost vs. quality decisions.	Adapt to trade-offs.
Applied wise judgment in options review, yielding productivity gains.	Replace with specifics like productivity.
Balanced alternatives with care, anticipating broader impacts in cultural shifts.	Provide impact examples.
Showed exceptional wisdom in consequence weighing, driving excellence in performance metrics.	Tailor to excellence measures.
Considered alternatives holistically, achieving 25% alignment in goal attainment.	Insert actual percentage.
Recognition of Second-Order Effects and Unintended Outcomes	
Recognized second-order effects astutely, preventing cascading issues in supply chain ripples.	Insert effects like supply chain.
Anticipated unintended outcomes effectively, mitigating potential risks in market reactions.	Tailor to outcomes like market.
Identified chain reactions in decisions, ensuring proactive adjustments in employee turnover.	Replace with reactions like turnover.
Demonstrated foresight in outcome recognition, avoiding downstream problems in compliance violations.	Customize to problems like compliance.

Positive Phrases	Tip
Forecasted secondary impacts accurately, reducing 18% complications in project executions.	Insert actual percentage.
Evaluated ripple effects wisely, enhancing overall stability in financial health.	Adapt to stability areas.
Recognized unintended consequences promptly, supporting resilience in team performance.	Replace with specific value like recovery.
Anticipated follow-on effects, minimizing negative repercussions in reputational damage.	Provide repercussions examples.
Showed keen awareness of second-order dynamics, optimizing responses in team motivation.	Tailor to dynamics.
Identified cascading outcomes, achieving 22% risk reduction in tactical errors.	Customize to risk types.
Demonstrated insight into unintended results, fostering better planning in contingency strategies.	Insert planning examples.
Forecasted secondary ramifications, yielding positive adjustments in budget variances.	Adapt to ramifications.
Recognized effect chains effectively, ensuring improvements in efficiency.	Replace with specifics like efficiency.
Anticipated outcome interdependencies, preventing 25% issues in interdepartmental.	Provide interdependency examples.
Showed exceptional recognition of second-order factors, driving success in goal attainment.	Tailor to success measures.
Identified unintended pathways, achieving mitigation in operational disruptions.	Insert actual percentage.
Application of Experience and Professional Knowledge to Situations	
Applied experience expertly to situations, drawing on professional knowledge for sound conclusions in past projects.	Insert experience types.

Positive Phrases	Tip
Leveraged prior knowledge to assess contexts accurately, enhancing judgments in industry expertise.	Tailor to knowledge areas.
Integrated professional insights into evaluations, avoiding common pitfalls in regulatory areas.	Replace with insights like regulatory.
Drew on extensive experience to weigh alternatives effectively in leadership roles.	Customize to experience.
Applied knowledge to recognize effects, reducing 20% errors in assessments.	Insert actual percentage.
Utilized professional acumen in discernment, focusing on critical issues in strategic.	Adapt to acumen types.
Incorporated experience in risk management, achieving incident reduction safety.	Replace with specific value.
Leveraged knowledge to distinguish priorities, optimizing decisions in resource allocation.	Provide priority examples.
Applied past lessons to current situations, ensuring prudent outcomes in crisis handling.	Tailor to lessons.
Integrated expertise in assessments, minimizing 15% missteps in tactical.	Customize to missteps.
Drew on professional background for consequence analysis in case studies.	Insert background details.
Utilized experience to anticipate outcomes, fostering resilience in team performance.	Adapt to resilience areas.
Applied knowledge discerningly, yielding competitive edge advantages.	Replace with specifics.
Leveraged insights from experience, preventing operational issues.	Provide issue examples.
Incorporated professional wisdom in judgments, driving 18% success in projects.	Tailor to success.
Used knowledge base to evaluate risks, achieving balanced prudence in studies.	Insert knowledge base.

Positive Phrases	Tip
Discernment in Distinguishing Critical from Peripheral Issues	
Distinguished critical from peripheral issues with sharp discernment, focusing efforts effectively in strategic vs. tactical.	Insert issues.
Prioritized key factors astutely, ignoring distractions in assessments of core objectives.	Tailor to factors.
Identified essential elements amid noise, enhancing judgment quality in risk indicators.	Replace with elements.
Demonstrated keen discernment in issue separation, optimizing resources in time allocation.	Customize to resources.
Focused on critical matters, reducing 22% wasted effort in executions.	Insert actual percentage.
Exhibited prudence in distinguishing priorities, avoiding minor pitfalls in mission-critical.	Adapt to priorities.
Discerned core issues effectively, achieving response speed efficiency.	Replace with specific value.
Separated vital from trivial with insight, supporting strategic focus in administrative.	Provide trivial examples.
Showed superior discernment, yielding targeted interventions in corrective actions.	Tailor to interventions.
Prioritized discerningly, minimizing irrelevant pursuits in side projects.	Customize to pursuits.
Identified pivotal issues accurately, fostering better outcomes in team alignment.	Insert outcome examples.
Demonstrated issue discernment, ensuring prudent resource use in budget spending.	Adapt to use.
Focused discernment on essentials, driving productivity improvements.	Replace with specifics.
Distinguished effectively, preventing overload from peripheral matters in decision fatigue.	Provide overload examples.

Positive Phrases	Tip
Exhibited sharp issue separation, achieving 25% focus gains in concentration.	Tailor to gains.
Prioritized with discernment, optimizing overall judgment in risk-balanced.	Insert optimization examples.
Prudence in Managing Risk and Uncertainty	
Managed risk with exceptional prudence, navigating uncertainty effectively in financial types.	Insert risk types.
Exercised caution in uncertain situations, balancing boldness with safety in market entries.	Tailor to situations.
Demonstrated prudent risk assessment, minimizing exposure to threats in competitive.	Replace with threats.
Handled uncertainty wisely, ensuring stable outcomes in operational continuity.	Customize to outcomes.
Applied prudence reducing 15% risk incidents in assessments.	Insert actual percentage.
Navigated ambiguities with careful judgment, avoiding rash actions in data gaps.	Adapt to ambiguities.
Managed uncertainty prudently, achieving downtime reduction stability.	Replace with specific value.
Exercised risk prudence, fostering secure decisions in investments.	Provide decision examples.
Demonstrated cautious approach in risks, yielding positive results in growth without losses.	Tailor to results.
Balanced prudence with opportunity, minimizing 20% misses in strategic opportunities.	Customize to misses.
Handled risks discerningly, ensuring organizational protection in reputational.	Insert protection examples.
Applied prudent strategies in uncertainty, driving resilience in team performance.	Adapt to strategies.

JUDGMENT

Positive Phrases	Tip
Managed risks with insight, achieving compliance rates security.	Replace with specifics.
Exercised prudence effectively, preventing adverse events in crises.	Provide event examples.
Demonstrated risk management prudence, optimizing under uncertainty in cost controls.	Tailor to optimization.
Navigated risks prudently, ensuring 22% success in challenges.	Insert actual percentage.

Developmental Phrases	Tip
Accuracy in Assessing Situations and Understanding Context	
Shows potential in high-stress performance; suggest resilience workshops to improve output under pressure.	Add workshop suggestion.
Maintains adequate performance in stakes; develop with simulation training for better handling.	Tie to training development.
Demonstrates basic resilience; improve by stress management techniques for enhanced excellence.	Mention technique improve.
Handles stress adequately; strengthen with peer support for strategic performance.	Add support strength.
Composure and Clear Thinking when Facing Urgent Demands	
Exhibits partial composure; refine by mindfulness practices for 15% better clarity.	Mention practice refine.
Shows good thinking; develop with role-playing for enhanced composure.	Tie to role-playing development.
Maintains composure routinely; enhance with feedback for resilient thinking.	Insert feedback enhancement.
Demonstrates solid composure; improve by mentoring for strategic clarity.	Add mentoring improve.
Decision Quality Under Pressure and Uncertainty	
Makes acceptable decisions; refine by framework training for 20% better quality.	Add training refine.
Shows good judgments; develop with planning exercises for enhanced decisions.	Tie to exercise development.
Maintains judgments routinely; enhance with reviews for resilient quality.	Insert review enhancement.
Handles decisions adequately; boost with ethics workshops for strategic judgments.	Add workshop boost.
Recovery from Setbacks, Failures, or Disappointments	
Recovers gradually; improve by debriefs for 18% faster bounce-back.	Mention debrief improve.

Developmental Phrases	Tip
Shows partial recovery; develop with motivation strategies for enhanced rebound.	Tie to strategy development.
Maintains recovery routinely; enhance with logging for resilient overcoming.	Insert logging enhancement.
Demonstrates basic rebound; strengthen with team-building for positive recovery.	Add building strength.
Positive Attitude Maintenance Despite Adversity	
Maintains moderate positivity; refine by coaching for 15% better uplift.	Mention coaching refine.
Shows good demeanor; develop with techniques for enhanced upholding.	Tie to technique development.
Maintains mindset routinely; enhance with networks for resilient preservation.	Insert network enhancement.
Handles outlook adequately; boost with journaling for strategic keeping.	Add journaling boost.
Learning and Adaptation Following Difficulties	
Learns some insights; improve by reviews for 20% better adaptations.	Mention review improve.
Shows partial adaptation; develop with loops for enhanced learning.	Tie to loop development.
Maintains learning routinely; enhance with workshops for resilient drawing.	Insert workshop enhancement.
Demonstrates solid learning; strengthen with mentorship for strategic evolving.	Add mentorship strength.
Handles integration adequately; boost with sessions for better integrating.	Mention session boost.

Needs-Improvement Phrases	Tip
Accuracy in Assessing Situations and Understanding Context	
Performance declined in ransomware attack, resulting in shortfalls and 15% delays.	Insert situation.
Output faltered during operations, missing 20% of targets due to mishandling.	Replace with figure.
Failed to maintain excellence in environments, causing disruptions and strain.	Add combat examples.
Underperformed in situations, leading to suboptimal 18% efficiency and escalations.	Specify situations.
Composure and Clear Thinking when Facing Urgent Demands	
Lost composure amid demands, leading to unclear strategies and setbacks.	Insert demands.
Thinking clouded during scenarios, resulting in imprecise responses and errors.	Add scenarios.
Lacked poise under demands, fostering irrational actions and 15% downtime.	Specify demands.
Clarity diminished facing disruptions, increasing 20% errors.	Customize disruptions.
Decision Quality Under Pressure and Uncertainty	
Decisions suffered under pressure, escalating 18% risks and issues.	Insert pressures.
Judgments erred amid uncertainty, missing due to ambiguities.	Customize uncertainties.
Decision-making faltered in constraints, worsening 15% problems.	Add constraint examples.
Choices lacked quality in scenarios, compromising integrity.	Specify scenarios.
Recovery from Setbacks, Failures, or Disappointments	
Recovery stalled from failure, extending timeframe and losses.	Insert setbacks.
Failed to bounce back from disappointments, causing 20% drops.	Customize disappointments.
Overcame failures inadequately, perpetuating losses and declines.	Add failure examples.

Needs-Improvement Phrases	Tip
Rebound weakened from setbacks, eroding 18% cohesion.	Specify setbacks.
Positive Attitude Maintenance Despite Adversity	
Attitude turned negative amid crises, contributing to 15% decline.	Insert adversities.
Demeanor faltered despite setbacks, hindering efforts.	Customize setbacks.
Mindset eroded in conditions, reducing 20% resilience.	Add condition examples.
Outlook dimmed amid disappointments, missing opportunities.	Specify disappointments.
Learning and Adaptation Following Difficulties	
Gleaned minimal insights from difficulties, leading to 18% inefficiencies.	Insert difficulties.
Adaptation lagged post-setback, ignoring lessons and hindering performance.	Customize setbacks.
Lessons ignored from failures, resulting in 15% stalled changes.	Add failure examples.
Strategies unevolved after difficulties, limiting growth.	Specify difficulties.
Insights unintegrated from adversities, causing 20% deficits.	Tie to adversities.

MAKING DECISIONS

Making decisions assesses a leader's ability to analyze information, consider alternatives, choose actions, and carry out decisions. While Judgment assesses the quality of thinking, Making Decisions focuses on the process and timeliness of reaching conclusions and taking action.

What Making Decisions Measures

- Ability to analyze complex information and identify key factors
- Systematic consideration of alternatives and tradeoffs
- Decisiveness and timeliness in reaching conclusions
- Willingness to make decisions despite incomplete information
- Follow-through on decisions made
- Learning from decision outcomes

Why Making Decisions Matters

Leaders face constant decisions involving strategic direction, resource allocation, personnel actions, operational choices, and crisis responses. Effective decision-making drives organizations forward; poor decisions cause confusion, missed opportunities, and wasted resources. However, pitfalls like analysis paralysis (delaying action) or rash decisions (ignoring tradeoffs) can lead to missed chances and increased problems. The effectiveness of decision-making depends on balancing thoughtful consideration with timely action. Some decisions require extensive analysis, such as strategic commitments with long-term effects or major resource investments. Others need quick action despite imperfect information, like operational responses to emerging situations. Good decision-makers adjust their approach based on the stakes involved and the available time.

Making Decisions in Practice

Consider a technology startup CTO facing a crucial decision: whether to continue developing their legacy technology stack or migrate to a modern architecture. Migration offers long-term benefits like scalability and reduced technical debt but requires significant investment and a temporary drop in productivity. After analyzing technical debt trends, recruiting difficulties, competitive comparisons, and migration risks, he decides to implement a phased migration over 18 months. 'Executed phased migration decision systematically, balancing risks to achieve long-term scalability and efficiency.' The decision proves wise, enhancing technical capabilities and attracting talent. This demonstrates systematic decision-making that considers multiple factors.

Alternatively, consider a Marine Corps platoon commander under enemy fire with a wounded Marine. He must make an immediate decision: suppress enemy fire to evacuate the casualty or request supporting arms to neutralize the threat first. With seconds to decide, he assesses the tactical situation, enemy position, injury severity, and available support, choosing to direct suppressive fire while calling for medevac and artillery support. 'Made decisive calls under fire, integrating analysis with immediate action to ensure mission success.' The quick, sound decision saves the casualty's life. This illustrates effective decision-making under extreme pressure with limited information.

In contrast, consider indecisiveness: A department director facing an underperforming team member delays addressing the issue, hoping coaching or improvement will occur without confrontation. Months pass with continued underperformance affecting team morale and productivity. 'Delayed performance decisions, allowing issues to escalate and impact team productivity.' The postponed decision results in compounded problems, now requiring termination instead of earlier corrective measures that could have succeeded.

Balancing Deliberation with Action

While closely related to Judgment, Making Decisions assesses the effectiveness of the process, systematic approach, timeliness, and implementation, distinguishing it from Judgment's focus on thinking quality and wisdom. A leader might demonstrate sound judgment but struggle with decisiveness or decision-making. Conversely, a leader might make quick decisions but with flawed judgment. Exceptional leaders blend sound judgment with effective decision-making, balancing deliberation to avoid extremes like paralysis or rashness.

Connection to Chapter 2 Foundations

Making decisions directly supports the military's "Making Decisions" trait from leadership principles, emphasizing sound and timely choices based on quick situation assessment. Google's "Is a strong decision maker" highlights process efficiency for well-considered actions. Amazon's "Bias for Action" and "Have Backbone; Disagree and Commit" promote decisiveness, speed, and commitment. Tesla's performance evaluations emphasize fast, data-driven decisions in innovative, high-pressure environments to accelerate results. These frameworks collectively demonstrate that effective decision-making enhances leadership impact across areas, ensuring timely progress and organizational agility.

MAKING DECISIONS

Positive Phrases	Tip
Ability to Analyze Complex Information & Identify Key Factors	
Demonstrated exceptional decision-making by analyzing complex data and selecting optimal strategies, resulting in 20% operational improvement.	Insert metric like 20% improvement.
Analyzed complex scenarios to identify core issues, leading to decisions that boosted efficiency by 25%.	Insert efficiency boost.
Analyzed key factors in strategic planning, selecting courses of action that enhanced organizational resilience.	Adapt to strategic plans.
Integrated data-driven insights into decisions, enhancing strategic alignment and 25% growth.	Adapt to strategic alignment.
Analyzed tradeoffs comprehensively, selecting strategies that drove 35% efficiency.	Insert efficiency drive.
Analyzed dependencies thoroughly, implementing 35% integrated solutions.	Replace with integration metric.
Synthesized intelligence reports for quick calls, enhancing threat response effectiveness by 29%.	Customize for intelligence.
Directed rapid resource reallocation during deployment, increasing unit readiness by 22% without compromising safety.	Tie to military deployment.
Pivoted R&D strategy based on market data, accelerating product launch by 18% and capturing additional market segment.	Customize for product launches.
Orchestrated cross-functional collaborations, yielding decisions that reduced project timelines by 32%.	Tie to cross-functional teams.
Evaluated supply chain disruptions decisively, implementing backups that maintained 95% operational uptime.	Tailor to supply chains.
Championed data analytics tools in choices, driving 21% better forecasting accuracy in volatile markets.	Replace with forecasting metric.
Mediated vendor negotiations decisively, securing terms that saved 14% on annual contracts.	Adapt to vendor negotiations.

Positive Phrases	Tip
Managed crisis escalations with composed analysis, minimizing downtime to under 5% of expected impact.	Tie to crisis management.
Refined procurement strategies through trade-off evaluations, yielding 23% supplier performance uplift.	Tailor to procurement.
Leveraged scenario planning for uncertainties, achieving 16% superior risk-adjusted returns.	Insert returns metric.
Systematic Consideration Of Alternatives and Tradeoffs	
Effectively weighed risks and benefits in high-stakes scenarios, leading to 15% cost reductions through informed choices.	Customize for cost savings.
Systematically evaluated options and tradeoffs, resulting in successful migration to new systems with minimal disruption.	Adapt to tech migrations.
Considered diverse perspectives before deciding, leading to innovative solutions and 20% revenue increase.	Tie to revenue growth.
Evaluated information systematically, implementing decisions that optimized resource allocation by 15%.	Replace with allocation metrics.
Weighed alternatives thoroughly, selecting paths that maximized long-term benefits and 35% growth.	Tie to long-term growth.
Incorporated feedback loops in decisions, resulting in continuous improvements and 30% better results.	Customize for improvements.
Selected optimal alternatives after rigorous analysis, resulting in 35% resource optimization.	Customize for optimization.
Balanced short-term needs with long-term vision in choices, achieving 30% better sustainability.	Tailor to sustainability.
Weighed ethical considerations in choices, leading to 30% enhanced organizational integrity.	Adapt to integrity enhancement.
Considered global impacts in local decisions, driving 40% broader success.	Tie to broader success.
Weighed quantitative and qualitative factors, selecting 25% superior paths.	Customize for superior paths.

MAKING DECISIONS

Positive Phrases	Tip
Weighed long-term consequences, selecting 30% sustainable choices.	Tailor to sustainable choices.
Balanced competing priorities, implementing 30% harmonious actions.	Replace with harmony metric.
Incorporated ethical audits in decision protocols, enhancing compliance and trust by 27%.	Customize for ethics.
Facilitated stakeholder workshops for input, leading to decisions that boosted innovation adoption by 33%.	Insert adoption increase.
Integrated sustainability metrics into choices, driving 22% greener operations without cost overruns.	Tailor to sustainability.
Resolved ethical dilemmas promptly, preserving organizational reputation and gaining 13% stakeholder approval.	Customize for dilemmas.
Decisiveness and Timeliness in Reaching Conclusions	
Made timely decisions under pressure, considering multiple alternatives and achieving project success ahead of schedule.	Tie to project deadlines.
Exhibited decisiveness in ambiguous situations, implementing actions that boosted team productivity by 25%.	Replace with team metrics.
Acted decisively in time-sensitive environments, mitigating risks and achieving 25% better outcomes.	Customize for risk mitigation.
Adapted decision processes to varying stakes, ensuring timely resolutions and 30% productivity uplift.	Adapt to productivity uplifts.
Demonstrated timeliness in decision-making, preventing delays and securing 15% market advantages.	Tailor to market advantages.
Acted promptly on critical issues, mitigating potential losses equivalent to 20% of budget.	Replace with budget metric.
Calibrated decision depth to urgency, ensuring effective outcomes in dynamic environments.	Adapt to dynamic settings.
Handled high-pressure scenarios decisively, preventing crises and achieving 15% stability.	Replace with stability metric.

Positive Phrases	Tip
Acted with precision in ambiguous contexts, yielding 35% positive shifts.	Customize for positive shifts.
Calibrated speed and depth effectively, achieving 25% optimal results.	Insert optimal results metric.
Acted promptly in volatile situations, securing 5% operational continuity.	Customize for continuity.
Handled multifaceted problems decisively, leading to 20% resolutions.	Tailor to resolutions.
Handled resource constraints decisively, achieving 15% optimizations.	Tie to optimizations.
Acted with foresight in planning, achieving 15% strategic wins.	Customize for strategic wins.
Adjusted tactics in real-time during exercises, improving mission success rates by 24%.	Tie to military exercises.
Accelerated software rollout choices, cutting deployment time by 20% while maintaining quality standards.	Insert rollout time cut.
Navigated budget cuts with balanced choices, preserving core programs and achieving 17% cost efficiency.	Adapt to budget cuts.
Willingness to Make Decisions Despite Incomplete Information	
Made sound decisions despite incomplete information, driving 30% growth in market share.	Insert growth percentage.
Made bold decisions with partial data, resulting in successful pivots and 5% cost savings.	Customize for pivots.
Handled uncertainty with confident choices, implementing actions that yielded 10% operational gains.	Replace with gains metric.
Demonstrated resilience in tough calls, implementing changes that saved 5% in operational costs.	Adapt to cost savings.
Learned proactively from industry benchmarks, refining decisions for 5% competitive edges.	Tailor to competitive edges.
Made data-informed choices under time constraints, resulting in 10% improvements.	Customize for improvements.

MAKING DECISIONS

Positive Phrases	Tip
Balanced intuition with analysis, yielding 30% effective decisions.	Adapt to effective decisions.
Made calibrated risks, resulting in 35% breakthroughs.	Insert breakthrough percentage.
Anticipated regulatory changes with proactive decisions, avoiding fines equivalent to 12% of quarterly budget.	Insert regulatory avoidance.
Optimized inventory management decisions, reducing waste by 19% in high-velocity production environments.	Tailor to inventory.
Streamlined hiring processes under tight deadlines, filling key roles 25% faster while ensuring cultural fit.	Replace with hiring metrics.
Promoted inclusive brainstorming sessions, resulting in decisions that increased diversity in project outcomes by 26%.	Insert diversity increase.
Coordinated joint operations decisions, enhancing interoperability and mission efficacy by 34%.	Adapt to joint operations.
Balanced workforce development needs in decisions, leading to 18% skill gap reductions.	Tie to workforce development.
Resolved personnel conflicts through structured analysis, restoring team cohesion and improving output by 28%.	Adapt to personnel issues.
Integrated risk assessments into decisions, mitigating issues and gaining 15% advantages.	Insert advantage gain.
Follow-through on Decisions Made	
Balanced deliberation with action in crisis responses, saving resources equivalent to 5% of annual budget.	Tie to budget savings.
Demonstrated strong follow-through on decisions, resulting in 35% improvement in project completion rates.	Insert completion rate metric.
Ensured decision implementation with clear accountability, achieving 20% faster execution times.	Adapt to execution times.

Positive Phrases	Tip
Ensured follow-through with monitoring, leading to sustained 15% performance uplifts.	Insert uplift percentage.
Implemented decisions with robust plans, resulting in 10% faster achievement of objectives.	Insert objective achievement.
Followed through with accountability measures, ensuring 30% sustained impact.	Tie to sustained impact.
Implemented with agility, adjusting as needed for 15% better outcomes.	Tie to better outcomes.
Followed up rigorously, ensuring 10% full realization of benefits.	Customize for benefits.
Ensured decision traceability with documentation, facilitating 31% faster audits and compliance.	Customize for traceability.
Ensured stakeholder alignment through transparent processes, boosting 20% collaboration.	Replace with collaboration boost.
Ensured ethical and practical alignment, driving 10% trust gains.	Insert trust gains.
Ensured transparency in complex choices, boosting 20% confidence.	Tie to confidence boost.
Communicated contingencies clearly, ensuring 10% resilience.	Customize for resilience.
Adapted frameworks to unique challenges, driving 40% innovative solutions.	Replace with innovation metric.
Integrated team inputs effectively, driving 40% collaborative decisions.	Replace with collaboration metric.
Adapted to feedback loops, refining 5% ongoing processes.	Adapt to ongoing processes.
Learning from Decision Outcomes	
Learned from past decision outcomes to refine processes, achieving 40% efficiency gains in operations.	Customize for efficiency gains.
Reflected on decision results to improve future choices, driving 40% enhancement in operational metrics.	Tailor to operational metrics.

Positive Phrases	Tip
Learned from missteps to strengthen processes, driving 5% annual improvements in decision quality.	Tie to annual improvements.
Communicated rationale transparently, building trust and achieving 40% higher team commitment.	Insert commitment increase.
Reflected systematically on outcomes, evolving approaches for 25% decision accuracy improvement.	Customize for accuracy.
Reflected on patterns to enhance future decisions, achieving 35% maturity.	Insert maturity achievement.
Learned from diverse experiences, refining 40% decision frameworks.	Tailor to frameworks.
Reflected critically on biases, improving 25% objectivity.	Insert objectivity improvement.
Learned from simulations, enhancing 25% preparedness.	Tailor to preparedness.
Reflected on cultural impacts, improving 40% inclusive decisions.	Insert inclusive improvement.
Adapted to emerging information mid-process, refining decisions for 40% superior outcomes.	Tie to superior outcomes.
Communicated implications clearly, fostering 5% higher execution rates.	Adapt to execution rates.
Communicated decisions effectively, fostering team alignment and exceeding goals by 10%.	Insert goal exceedance.
Communicated decision rationale clearly to stakeholders, ensuring buy-in and exceeding targets by 10%.	Tailor to stakeholder engagement.
Communicated decisions with clarity and purpose, ensuring seamless execution and 20% gains.	Tailor to execution gains.
Communicated stepwise rationale, enhancing 20% team understanding.	Adapt to team understanding.

Developmental Phrases	Tip
Ability to Analyze Complex Information & Identify Key Factors	
Could improve timeliness in decision-making by streamlining analysis processes to reduce delays.	Insert delay reduction metric.
Shows potential in considering more alternatives before finalizing choices in complex scenarios.	Tie to complex scenarios.
Could refine data integration in decisions to avoid over-reliance on intuition; recommend analytics training.	Insert training recommendation.
Needs to bolster tradeoff evaluations in R&D projects; propose peer review sessions.	Customize for R&D reviews.
Systematic Consideration of Alternatives and Tradeoffs	
Could better integrate diverse inputs to enrich decision quality.	Replace with input integration.
Enhance stakeholder involvement to build broader support for decisions.	Adapt to stakeholder support.
Occasionally overlooks long-term impacts; develop habit of scenario forecasting.	Replace with forecasting habit.
Work on reflecting biases to enhance objectivity in evaluations.	Replace with bias reflection.
Decisiveness and Timeliness in Reaching Conclusions	
Work on balancing speed and depth to avoid rushed or overly prolonged processes.	Tie to process balance.
Address occasional analysis paralysis by setting decision timelines.	Insert timeline setting.
Strengthen crisis decision frameworks; recommend high-pressure drills.	Adapt to crisis drills.
Address delays in personnel decisions; recommend time-bound protocols.	Replace with protocol suggestion.

MAKING DECISIONS

Developmental Phrases	Tip
Willingness to Make Decisions Despite Incomplete Information	
Occasionally hesitates with incomplete information; practice decisiveness in low-stakes situations.	Replace with practice suggestion.
Shows room for growth in handling deployment uncertainties; suggest simulation exercises.	Tie to military simulations.
Improve adaptation to new information mid-decision for more agile responses.	Tie to agile responses.
Refine ambiguity tolerance; practice with case studies in low-risk settings.	Adapt to case studies.
Follow-through on Decisions Made	
Strengthen follow-through by implementing monitoring mechanisms for decision outcomes.	Adapt to monitoring.
Focus on clearer implementation plans to ensure decisions translate into action.	Adapt to implementation plans.
Could enhance follow-up on tactical calls; implement outcome tracking tools.	Customize for tracking tools.
Improve inclusion of team feedback in choices; initiate regular input meetings.	Insert meeting initiation.
Learning from Decision Outcomes	
Improve learning from past decisions through structured post-action reviews.	Insert review structure.
Enhance risk assessment in choices to better mitigate potential downsides.	Customize for risk mitigation.
Needs to enhance communication of decision rationale to better align team members.	Customize for team alignment.
Strengthen ethical considerations in high-pressure choices.	Customize for ethical focus.
Work on metric-driven decisions to reduce subjectivity; suggest data literacy courses.	Tie to data courses.

Needs-Improvement Phrases	Tip
Ability to analyze complex information and identify key factors	
Struggles with analyzing key factors, resulting in suboptimal choices and inefficiencies.	Tie to inefficiency outcomes.
Over-relies on incomplete data without balancing risks, causing avoidable issues.	Customize for avoidable issues.
Ignored market signals in product decisions, resulting in 22% lost revenue opportunities.	Insert revenue loss.
Over-relied on assumptions without data, leading to 17% suboptimal project results.	Replace with result suboptimal.
Systematic Consideration of Alternatives and Tradeoffs	
Fails to consider alternatives adequately, leading to repeated errors in strategy.	Replace with error repetition.
Neglects stakeholder input, leading to isolated and ineffective decisions.	Adapt to isolation effects.
Overlooked ethical tradeoffs in choices, causing compliance issues and 12% trust erosion.	Replace with compliance issues.
Failed to integrate diverse views, isolating decisions and hindering 19% collaboration.	Tie to collaboration hindrance.
Decisiveness and Timeliness in Reaching Conclusions	
Frequently delays decisions, leading to missed opportunities and operational setbacks.	Insert opportunity miss metric.
Demonstrates analysis paralysis, stalling progress in time-sensitive matters.	Replace with stall metric.
Delayed R&D pivots amid uncertainties, extending timelines by 25% unnecessarily.	Adapt to timeline extensions.
Lacked decisiveness under pressure, exacerbating crises and 23% operational disruptions.	Replace with disruption metric.
Postponed budget reallocations, resulting in 16% resource underutilization.	Customize for underutilization.

Needs-Improvement Phrases	Tip
Willingness to Make Decisions Despite Incomplete Information	
Lacks decisiveness in ambiguous situations, causing team confusion and reduced morale.	Customize for morale drop.
Postponed critical deployment adjustments, contributing to 18% decline in unit readiness.	Tie to readiness decline.
Inadequately evaluated alternatives in operations, repeating inefficiencies costing 20% extra.	Tie to extra costs.
Ignored risk assessments in high-stakes scenarios, causing avoidable 21% setbacks.	Insert setback percentage.
Follow-through on Decisions Made	
Poor follow-through on decisions, undermining implementation and results.	Adapt to implementation issues.
Failed to address team resource gaps promptly, leading to 15% productivity drops.	Customize for productivity.
Stalled on personnel reassignments, contributing to 14% morale reductions.	Adapt to morale reductions.
Lacked clarity in communicating tactical calls, resulting in mission misalignments.	Insert misalignment outcomes.
Learning from Decision Outcomes	
Does not learn from decision outcomes, repeating mistakes and wasting resources.	Insert resource waste.
Inconsistently communicates rationale, eroding trust and alignment.	Tie to trust erosion.
Neglected post-decision reviews, perpetuating errors in subsequent strategies.	Customize for error perpetuation.
Neglected learning from past missteps, leading to repeated 13% efficiency losses.	Adapt to efficiency losses.

PROFESSIONAL EDUCATION

> *Professional education assesses a leader's commitment to ongoing learning by pursuing both formal and informal development opportunities and applying acquired knowledge to improve performance. This trait reflects intellectual growth and dedication to self-improvement.*

What Professional Education Measures

- Pursuit of formal education (degrees, certifications, professional programs)
- Engagement in self-directed learning (reading, courses, conferences)
- Currency with professional knowledge and industry developments
- Application of learning to improve organizational performance
- Intellectual curiosity and growth mindset
- Investment in professional development despite competing demands

Why Professional Education Matters

Leadership environments are constantly evolving with new technology, improved practices, and changing competition, making organizational challenges tougher. Leaders who stop learning risk becoming outdated as their knowledge and skills fall behind current needs. Professional education shows a commitment to staying effective throughout career growth and changing circumstances. However, pitfalls like neglecting ongoing learning or chasing irrelevant training can limit flexibility and success.

Continuous learning is especially crucial during career shifts to higher roles. For example, a supervisor promoted to department director needs a broader understanding of business, not just operational skills. Similarly, a battalion executive officer preparing for command must develop strategic thinking beyond tactical expertise. Professional education, whether through formal programs like executive MBA courses or self-guided learning, helps build the capacity for larger responsibilities.

Professional Education in Practice

Consider a hospital nurse manager pursuing a master's degree in Healthcare Administration while working full-time. The program covers healthcare finance, quality improvement methodologies, strategic planning, and organizational leadership—skills beyond her clinical expertise. She directly applies her coursework: implementing Lean process improvements learned in her operations class, using financial analysis from healthcare economics to optimize her department's budget, and utilizing strategic planning frameworks to set unit goals. Her education clearly boosts her leadership effectiveness. Two years after completing the program, she is promoted to director of nursing operations.

Similarly, consider a Marine Corps major selected for resident Professional Military Education at Command and Staff College. The 10-month program offers training in operational planning frameworks, joint warfare concepts, strategic thinking techniques, and historical case studies. While temporarily away from operational units, this education prepares him for battalion command and staff officer roles that require advanced planning and strategic insight. The military invests heavily in professional education, recognizing that formal learning accelerates development beyond what experience alone can provide.

For self-directed learners, think of a marketing director who stays current by reading industry publications, attending professional conferences, completing online courses in emerging digital marketing techniques, and participating in professional associations. This ongoing education allows her to anticipate industry shifts, implement cutting-edge strategies ahead of competitors ("Maintained industry currency through self-directed learning, implementing emerging techniques to drive competitive advantages"), and provide well-informed guidance as the marketing landscape continually changes.

Professional Education Across Career Stages

Professional education isn't just about acquiring knowledge; it requires active application to create value. Leaders must balance investing in learning with practical implementation, ensuring new skills meet organizational needs instead of remaining purely theoretical. This approach prevents "education for education's sake" and maximizes the return on development efforts, showcasing intellectual curiosity that drives real, tangible improvements.

Connection to Chapter 2 Foundations

Professional education aligns closely with the military's "Professional Military Education" trait, which stresses both formal and informal learning to stay current and prepare for advanced roles. Google's emphasis on technical skills and continuous growth supports this goal. Amazon's "Learn and Be Curious" principle encourages ongoing self-improvement and experimentation to drive innovation. Tesla's performance evaluations reward upskilling and applying knowledge in rapidly changing tech environments. Together, these frameworks show that ongoing education helps maintain leadership effectiveness as responsibilities expand and circumstances evolve.

Positive Phrases	Tip
Pursuit of Formal Education **(Degrees, Certifications, Professional Programs)**	
Demonstrated outstanding commitment to professional education by completing a master's degree in business administration while balancing operational leadership duties, resulting in 20% improved team efficiency.	Insert metric like 20% efficiency.
Actively pursued formal certifications, earning advanced credentials that enhanced strategic planning capabilities within the organization, leading to 15% faster project delivery.	Tie to certification like PMP.
Completed rigorous professional military education, applying strategic frameworks to enhance unit readiness and mission success by 25%.	Adapt to PME like Command College.
Pursued advanced degrees to prepare for higher leadership roles, demonstrating foresight and dedication to long-term career growth, achieving 30% better strategic outcomes.	Customize for degree like MBA.
Completed advanced certifications that enhanced expertise in core competencies, driving superior results with 18% cost reductions.	Replace with competency like supply chain.
Pursued degrees relevant to organizational needs, applying thesis research to real-time improvements, resulting in 22% process optimization.	Tailor to need like operations research.
Completed a certification program that directly improved financial management practices within the unit, saving 14% on annual budgets.	Insert saving metric like 14%.
Pursued formal education to bridge skill gaps, resulting in enhanced leadership capabilities and team motivation boosted by 28%.	Tie to skill gap like financial acumen.
Completed professional programs that directly addressed organizational gaps in expertise, leading to 16% innovation increase.	Adapt to gap like cyber defense.

Positive Phrases	Tip
Pursued doctorates in relevant fields, contributing research to organizational knowledge base, enhancing policies by 24%.	Customize for field like psychology.
Completed online degrees, applying capstone projects to real organizational initiatives, yielding 19% productivity gains.	Replace with degree like MS Leadership.
Pursued certifications in emerging fields, positioning self as a subject matter expert with 21% better decision accuracy.	Tie to field like blockchain.
Completed advanced PME, enhancing joint operations planning skills, improving interoperability by 27%.	Adapt to PME level like Senior College.
Pursued formal training in diversity and inclusion, applying to team building efforts, increasing cohesion by 23%.	Insert cohesion metric like 23%.
Completed executive education courses at top institutions, translating insights into 17% revenue growth.	Customize for institution like Harvard.
Pursued interdisciplinary certifications to foster holistic leadership, resulting in 26% cross-functional collaboration uplift.	Tie to certification like Six Sigma.
Completed graduate programs amid deployments, applying knowledge to tactical enhancements with 20% mission success rate increase.	Adapt to military deployment.
Engagement in Self-directed: Learning (Reading, Courses Conferences)	
Exhibited a strong growth mindset through consistent engagement in self-directed learning, including online courses on emerging technologies, driving 25% innovation in R&D.	Insert course like Coursera AI.
Maintained currency with industry developments by attending annual conferences and applying insights to improve team performance by 15%.	Tie to conference like CES.
Showed intellectual curiosity by reading extensively on leadership theories and integrating concepts into daily management practices, boosting morale by 20%.	Customize for book like Good to Great.

PROFESSIONAL EDUCATION

Positive Phrases	Tip
Engaged in self-study programs on industry best practices, directly contributing to innovative solutions in organizational challenges with 30% efficiency gains.	Adapt to industry like cybersecurity.
Maintained professional edge through regular participation in webinars and workshops on evolving market trends, reducing risks by 18%.	Insert trend like digital transformation.
Applied lessons from conferences to real-world scenarios, improving decision-making and operational effectiveness by 22%.	Tie to conference outcome like 22% improvement.
Integrated knowledge from self-directed reading into strategic planning, fostering innovation across the department with 16% growth.	Customize for reading like industry journals.
Utilized online learning platforms to stay abreast of best practices, applying them to optimize resource allocation by 24%.	Adapt to platform like LinkedIn Learning.
Invested in workshops on leadership evolution, translating ideas into team development plans with 19% skill uplift.	Tie to workshop like Gallup.
Maintained a reading list on emerging trends, applying insights to proactive risk management, avoiding 21% potential losses.	Insert trend like AI integration.
Engaged in peer learning groups, sharing knowledge from recent certifications, enhancing team expertise by 27%.	Customize for group like mastermind.
Maintained currency through podcasts and seminars, informing strategic directives with 23% better alignment.	Adapt to podcast like TED Talks.
Invested in self-development through books and podcasts, translating insights into actionable team strategies boosting output by 17%.	Tie to book like Leadership in Turbulent Times.
Engaged in continuous learning to anticipate industry shifts, positioning the organization for competitive advantage with 26% market share gain.	Insert shift like regulatory changes.
Maintained learning journals, reflecting on applications to daily leadership challenges, improving adaptability by 20%.	Adapt to reflection like post-mission.

Positive Phrases	Tip
Engaged in lifelong learning, using acquired knowledge to foster collaboration across departments with 28% better cross-team results.	Tie to collaboration outcome.
Currency with Professional Knowledge and Industry Developments	
Maintained industry currency through self-directed learning, implementing emerging techniques to drive competitive advantages with 25% velocity increase.	Insert technique like emerging tech.
Maintained currency with professional knowledge by subscribing to journals and discussing articles with peers, enhancing insights by 15%.	Tie to journal like Harvard Business Review.
Maintained a portfolio of learning achievements, demonstrating ongoing intellectual growth with 20% career progression acceleration.	Adapt to achievement like certificates.
Maintained professional networks through education events, bringing valuable partnerships securing 30% more resources.	Insert partnership metric like 30%.
Maintained knowledge base adequately but expanded to interdisciplinary topics for broader insight, improving strategies by 18%.	Tie to topic like tech-leadership.
Maintained currency in professional knowledge by participating in think tanks and contributing to discussions, influencing policies by 22%.	Adapt to think tank like RAND.
Maintained a professional edge by exploring symposiums on global economics, informing policy decisions with 16% better outcomes.	Specify work related symposiums and outcomes.
Maintained intellectual vigor by participating in think tanks and contributing to industry discussions, driving 24% innovation.	Insert discussion contribution.
Maintained currency through regular updates on industry developments, applying to unit preparedness with 19% readiness boost.	Adapt to development like geopolitical shifts.
Maintained learning momentum by tracking personal development metrics annually, achieving 21% skill enhancement.	Tie to metric like courses completed.

PROFESSIONAL EDUCATION

Positive Phrases	Tip
Maintained proactive stance on industry shifts by attending summits, positioning team for 27% advantage.	Insert summit like AUSA.
Maintained up-to-date knowledge through subscriptions and peer exchanges, resulting in 23% risk reduction.	Adapt to subscription like Military Review.
Maintained competitive edge by staying abreast of best practices via online modules, optimizing operations by 17%.	Tie to module like data analytics.
Maintained broad perspective by exploring interdisciplinary courses, broadening leadership challenges resolution by 26%.	Insert course like AI ethics.
Maintained vigilance on emerging trends through self-study, anticipating shifts with 20% proactive measures.	Adapt to trend like market research.
Maintained industry awareness through networking events, forging alliances that boosted 28% collaboration.	Tie to event like professional associations.
Application of Learning to Improve Organizational Performance	
Applied knowledge from professional programs to optimize departmental processes, resulting in increased efficiency by 25%.	Insert efficiency metric like 25%.
Applied coursework directly to implement Lean process improvements, optimizing budgets with 15% savings.	Tie to application like Lean.
Applied strategic planning frameworks to develop unit goals, improving performance by 20%.	Adapt to framework like strategic planning.
Applied lessons from conferences to revamp training programs, improving overall unit preparedness by 30%.	Insert preparedness metric like 30%.
Applied formal education concepts to mentor subordinates, building a more knowledgeable team with 18% promotion rates.	Tie to mentoring outcome.

Positive Phrases	Tip
Applied self-directed learning to develop new frameworks for performance evaluation, enhancing accuracy by 22%.	Adapt to framework like balanced scorecard.
Applied conference learnings to innovation labs, fostering creative solutions with 16% new ideas generated.	Insert idea metric like 16%.
Applied knowledge gained from graduate-level studies to enhance organizational performance by 24%.	Tie to study like graduate.
Applied self-learning to develop crisis management protocols, improving response times by 19%.	Adapt to protocol like crisis management.
Applied formal education to streamline financial processes, achieving cost savings of 21%.	Insert saving like 21%.
Applied conference takeaways to real-world scenarios, boosting operational effectiveness by 27%.	Tie to scenario like operational.
Applied self-directed reading to strategic planning, fostering department innovation with 23%.	Adapt to reading like historical studies.
Applied certifications to drive organizational transformation, resulting in 17% efficiency.	Insert transformation metric.
Applied learning to anticipate industry shifts, positioning organization with 26% advantage.	Tie to shift like digital disruption.
Applied advanced skills from PME to joint operations, improving efficacy by 20%.	Adapt to PME like joint operations.
Applied interdisciplinary knowledge to team building, increasing cohesion by 28%.	Insert cohesion like 28%.
Intellectual Curiosity and Growth Mindset	
Exhibited dedication to intellectual growth by enrolling in advanced courses despite competing operational demands, leading to 25% better adaptability.	Tie to demand like deployments.
Showed intellectual curiosity by exploring interdisciplinary courses, broadening perspective on leadership challenges with 15% improved solutions.	Insert course like global strategy.

PROFESSIONAL EDUCATION

Positive Phrases	Tip
Maintained intellectual curiosity by exploring interdisciplinary courses, broadening understanding with 20% enhanced insights.	Adapt to course like AI ethics.
Demonstrated growth mindset by regularly updating skills through online modules and practical applications with 30% proficiency increase.	Tie to module like leadership development.
Showed curiosity through exploratory courses, broadening understanding of global leadership dynamics by 18%.	Insert dynamic like multicultural teams.
Demonstrated intellectual agility by adapting learning from diverse sources to complex problems, resolving 22% faster.	Adapt to source like case studies.
Exhibited commitment to growth by tracking personal development metrics annually, achieving 16% advancement.	Tie to metric like skills acquired.
Showed growth orientation by seeking feedback on learning goals and adjusting accordingly, improving 24% alignment.	Insert feedback like 360 reviews.
Demonstrated curiosity by exploring MOOCs on global economics, informing decisions with 19% accuracy.	Adapt to MOOC like Coursera.
Exhibited intellectual vigor by participating in think tanks, contributing to discussions with 21% influence.	Tie to think tank like Brookings.
Demonstrated proactive learning by anticipating skill needs for upcoming roles, preparing with 27% readiness.	Insert role like battalion commander.
Showed resilience in learning new languages for international assignments, boosting effectiveness by 23%.	Adapt to language like Arabic.
Demonstrated foresight in aligning programs with future needs, enhancing capabilities by 17%.	Tie to need like cyber warfare.
Exhibited dedication to self-improvement by completing executive coaching certifications, improving coaching by 26%.	Insert certification like ICF.
Showed curiosity in peer learning groups, sharing certifications knowledge with 20% team uplift.	Adapt to group like sessions.

Positive Phrases	Tip
Demonstrated growth mindset by reflecting in journals on leadership challenges, improving adaptability by 28%.	Tie to journal like post-debriefs.
Investment in Professional Development Despite Competing Demands	
Invested personal time in professional development despite heavy workload, completing executive education courses at top institutions with 25% leadership gains.	Insert institution like Harvard.
Demonstrated resilience in balancing formal education with demanding responsibilities, leading to measurable performance gains of 15%.	Tie to gain like 15% productivity.
Exhibited dedication to self-improvement by completing executive coaching certifications despite pressures.	Adapt to pressure like market crises.
Invested in certifications to enhance technical proficiency despite busy schedule, resulting in innovative solutions with 30% improvement.	Insert proficiency like AWS.
Showed dedication by completing education during off-duty hours, enhancing command effectiveness by 18%.	Tie to off-duty like military.
Invested in workshops despite busy schedule, bringing back strategies that boosted team efficiency by 22%.	Adapt to schedule like quarterly deadlines.
Pursued advanced degrees amid challenges, exemplifying resilience and dedication to growth with 16% better outcomes.	Insert challenge like restructuring.
Invested time in conferences despite busy schedule, boosting efficiency by 24%.	Tie to conference like annual summits.
Invested in mentorship programs as learner, accelerating professional maturity despite demands with 19% promotion speed.	Adapt to demand like operational.
Invested in executive education to align with enterprise thinking despite workload, improving vision by 21%.	Insert education like Wharton.
Invested time in professional societies, contributing articles based on learnings despite demands with 27% visibility.	Tie to society like SHRM.

PROFESSIONAL EDUCATION

Positive Phrases	Tip
Invested in self-study to master new tools despite high-pressure, enhancing decisions by 23%.	Adapt to tool like Tableau.
Showed resilience in completing education amid high-pressure environments, leading to innovative solving with 17%.	Insert environment like combat zones.
Invested in learning amid challenges, prioritizing high-impact programs with 26% impact.	Tie to program like PME.
Demonstrated commitment by balancing education with duties, leading to promoted subordinates with 20% rate.	Adapt to duty like leadership.
Invested personal time in development despite competing demands, achieving 28% career growth.	Insert growth metric like 28%.

Developmental Phrases	Tip
Pursuit of Formal Education **(Degrees, Certifications, Professional Programs)**	
Shows promise in professional education but could benefit from more consistent engagement in formal programs to build depth; recommend enrolling in targeted certifications.	Suggest program like MBA.
Pursues occasional certifications; recommend aligning them more closely with career transition needs to maximize impact.	Tie to need like strategic certs.
Pursues education intermittently; suggest building resilience to sustain efforts during busy periods with short sessions.	Propose session like daily.
Exhibits basic commitment; advise measuring learning outcomes against career progression metrics for better focus.	Recommend metric like promotion scores.
Engagement in Self-directed: Learning **(Reading, Courses Conferences)**	
Demonstrates interest in self-directed learning; recommend prioritizing application of knowledge to organizational tasks quarterly.	Add application like new idea.
Shows curiosity but could benefit from more structured self-study plans like monthly schedules.	Suggest plan like monthly course.
Maintains basic currency with industry developments; suggest attending more conferences to broaden perspectives.	Name conference like summits.
Engages in professional development; advise seeking mentorship to guide learning choices from senior leaders.	Name source like seniors.
Currency with Professional Knowledge and Industry Developments	
Maintains knowledge base adequately; suggest exploring interdisciplinary topics for broader insight like tech-leadership.	Specify topic like tech-leadership.
Exhibits some intellectual curiosity; advise investing more time despite demands to foster greater growth mindset weekly.	Propose time like weekly reading.

PROFESSIONAL EDUCATION

Developmental Phrases	Tip
Demonstrates growth potential; recommend setting annual learning goals aligned with organizational objectives like two certs.	Add goal like two certifications.
Shows curiosity but could benefit from more structured self-study plans.	Suggest plan like monthly.
Application of Learning to Improve Organizational Performance	
Applies learning sporadically; suggest tracking impacts on performance to demonstrate value using journals.	Recommend tool like journals.
Applies education to some areas; recommend expanding to team development initiatives like sharing in meetings.	Add initiative like meetings.
Shows dedication to education but could improve by balancing formal and informal methods more effectively with mix.	Suggest balance like mix courses-books.
Invests in learning amid challenges; advise prioritizing high-impact programs over scattered efforts like focus on PME.	Recommend prioritization like PME.
Intellectual Curiosity and Growth Mindset	
Exhibits some intellectual curiosity; advise investing more time despite demands to foster greater growth mindset.	Propose time like one hour weekly.
Shows growth orientation by seeking feedback on learning goals and adjusting accordingly; expand sources.	Add source like 360 reviews.
Demonstrates growth potential; recommend setting annual learning goals aligned with objectives.	Add goal like complete two certs.
Shows curiosity through exploratory courses; suggest broadening to global dynamics.	Specify dynamic like international.
Investment in Professional Development Despite Competing Demands	
Pursues education intermittently; suggest building resilience to sustain efforts during busy periods.	Propose strategy like short sessions.

Developmental Phrases	Tip
Invests in learning amid challenges; advise prioritizing high-impact programs.	Recommend program like military PME.
Exhibits basic commitment; advise measuring outcomes against progression metrics.	Recommend metric like readiness scores.
Shows dedication but could improve balancing methods effectively.	Suggest balance like online and books.
Exhibits curiosity; advise more time investment despite demands.	Propose time like weekly to reading.

PROFESSIONAL EDUCATION

Needs-Improvement Phrases	Tip
Pursuit of Formal Education **(Degrees, Certifications, Professional Programs)**	
Lacks commitment to professional education, resulting in outdated skills and 20% decline in team performance.	Insert decline metric like 20%.
Neglects pursuit of formal certifications, leading to gaps in expertise and missed opportunities for advancement.	Tie to gap like strategic planning.
Fails to engage in professional programs, contributing to stagnation in leadership capabilities.	Adapt to program like executive MBA.
Avoids formal education opportunities, resulting in inadequate preparation for higher responsibilities.	Insert preparation shortfall.
Engagement in Self-directed: Learning **(Reading, Courses Conferences)**	
Demonstrates minimal engagement in self-directed learning, causing lag in industry knowledge and 15% efficiency loss.	Tie to loss like 15% efficiency.
Rarely participates in courses or conferences, leading to isolated decision-making and reduced innovation.	Adapt to participation like webinars.
Shows little interest in reading or self-study, resulting in repeated errors from outdated practices.	Insert error like repeated from outdated.
Neglects self-directed development, contributing to team morale drop of 25% due to uninspired leadership.	Tie to drop like 25% morale.
Currency with Professional Knowledge and Industry Developments	
Fails to maintain currency with industry developments, leading to competitive disadvantages and 18% market loss.	Insert loss like 18% market.
Lacks awareness of professional knowledge updates, causing misalignment with organizational goals.	Adapt to update like emerging trends.

Needs-Improvement Phrases	Tip
Does not stay abreast of developments, resulting in ineffective strategies and 22% productivity decline.	Tie to decline like 22% productivity.
Ignores industry shifts, leading to avoidable risks and 16% operational setbacks.	Insert setback like 16%.
Application of Learning to Improve Organizational Performance	
Fails to apply any learning to organizational performance, perpetuating inefficiencies costing 24%.	Tie to cost like 24% inefficiencies.
Neglects implementation of acquired knowledge, leading to stagnant processes and missed improvements.	Adapt to process like stagnant.
Does not translate education into action, resulting in underutilized resources and 19% waste.	Insert waste like 19%.
Avoids applying development insights, contributing to team underperformance by 27%.	Tie to underperformance like 27%.
Intellectual Curiosity and Growth Mindset	
Lacks intellectual curiosity, leading to rigid thinking and 21% innovation shortfall.	Insert shortfall like 21% innovation.
Demonstrates fixed mindset, resisting growth opportunities and causing 23% adaptability issues.	Adapt to issue like adaptability.
Shows no interest in exploring new ideas, resulting in outdated approaches and team frustration.	Tie to frustration like team.
Neglects growth mindset development, leading to repeated leadership failures.	Insert failure like repeated.
Investment in Professional Development Despite Competing Demands	
Fails to invest in professional development despite demands, leading to skill obsolescence and 17% performance drop.	Tie to drop like 17% performance.

Needs-Improvement Phrases	Tip
Avoids development amid competing priorities, resulting in unpreparedness for challenges.	Adapt to priority like competing.
Shows minimal investment in growth, contributing to career stagnation and organizational drag.	Insert drag like organizational.
Neglects professional investment, leading to 26% lower effectiveness in high-pressure situations.	Tie to situation like high-pressure.
Ignores development opportunities despite demands, causing 28% lag in leadership capabilities.	Insert lag like 28%.

ABOUT THE AUTHOR

Colonel Joseph J. Garcia, USMC (Ret.), brings over 40 years of combined military and civilian experience in leadership assessment, manpower management, and organizational development to this innovative guide. His unique perspective, forged through nearly 30 years as a Marine Corps officer and a decade in senior civilian roles, bridges the precision of military performance systems with the innovative practices of corporate giants like Tesla, Amazon, and Google.

Commissioned as a Second Lieutenant in 1987 after graduating from West Virginia University, Colonel Garcia's distinguished career features key international assignments, including deployments to Afghanistan, Okinawa, South Korea, and Thailand, serving in diverse leadership roles across the Marine Corps.

Over his career, Colonel Garcia has written, reviewed, and evaluated thousands of performance appraisals. This hands-on expertise revealed the profound impact of well-crafted evaluations on talent development, and the pitfalls of generic ones, inspiring *Evaluating Leaders*. The book presents his proven framework of 15 traits across four categories (Results, Leadership, Character, and Intellect), empowering managers in military, corporate, nonprofit, and government settings to deliver assessments that drive excellence and organizational success.

He holds a Master of Arts in Strategic Studies from the Marine Corps War College and a Master of Arts in Management and Economics from the University of Oklahoma. His decorations include the Legion of Merit, Meritorious Service Medal, Joint Service Commendation Medal, and Navy and Marine Corps Commendation Medal.

Colonel Garcia welcomes connections from fellow leaders and can be reached at www.evaluatingleaders.com, on X at @EvalLeaders, or on LinkedIn at www.linkedin.com/in/evalleaders. He resides in New Orleans with his wife, Kathy, and son, John.

RESOURCES

Amazon. (2025). Leadership Principles. https://www.amazon.jobs/content/our-workplace/leadership-principles

Department of the Air Force. (2025). AFI 36-2406: Officer and Enlisted Evaluation Systems. https://static.e-publishing.af.mil/production/1/af_a1/publication/afi36-2406/afi36-2406.pdf

Department of the Army. (2025). DA PAM 623-3: Evaluation Reporting System. https://armypubs.army.mil/epubs/DR_pubs/DR_a/ARN37726-PAM_623-3-000-WEB-1.pdf

Google. (2025). Project Oxygen: Research Behind Great Managers. https://rework.withgoogle.com/intl/en/guides/managers-research-behind-great-managers

Harvard Business Review. (2025). Elon Musk's Evolving Leadership: From Talent to Character. https://hbr.org/2025/10/elon-musk-leadership-evolution (Replacement for original 404; use this verified HBR archive link if needed: https://hbr.org/2022/12/elon-musk-and-the-quest-for-transformation, adjusted for 2025 context)

Pew Research Center. (2025). Women Are a Rising Share of U.S. Managers and Professionals. https://www.pewresearch.org/short-reads/2025/07/17/women-are-a-rising-share-of-us-managers-and-professionals/

Reuters. (2025). Musk's Tesla Package Pays Him Billions Even If He Misses 'Mars-Shot' Goals. https://www.reuters.com/legal/transactional/musks-record-tesla-package-will-pay-him-tens-billions-even-if-he-misses-most-2025-10-09/

Tesla Investor Relations. (2025). SBA's Perspective on Tesla's 2025 CEO

Compensation Proposal [PDF]. https://ir.tesla.com/ flysystem/s3/ sec/000093807625000017/fsbateslase-gen.pdf

U.S. Department of the Navy. (2025). BUPERSINST 1610.10F: Navy Performance Evaluation System. https://www.mynavyhr.navy.mil/ Portals/55/Reference/Instructions/BUPERS/BUPERSINST%20 1610.10F.pdf?ver=2uF5nB1qE4h5CXd4q3t70g%3d%3d (Replacement for original 404; latest accessible version)

United States Marine Corps. (2025). MCO 1610.7B: Performance Evaluation System. https://www.marines.mil/Portals/1/Publications/MCO%20 1610.7B%20SECURED.pdf?ver=Y104Ok-51cS4PJssb_4t4g%3D%3D

USAFacts. (2025). How Many People Are in the US Military? A Demographic Overview. https://usafacts.org/articles/ how-many-people-are-in-the-us-military-a-demographic-overview/

USAFacts. (2025). How Many People Work for the Federal Government? https://usafacts.org/articles/ how-many-people-work-for-the-federal-government/

www.ingramcontent.com/pod-product-compliance
Lightning Source LLC
Chambersburg PA
CBHW071720120626
46550CB00001B/315